Thomson Round Hall Nutshells

Constitutional Law
(Second Edition)

Thomson Round Hall Nutshells

Constitutional Law
(Second Edition)

Fergus W. Ryan

SERIES EDITOR
Bruce Carolan

ROUND HALL

THOMSON REUTERS

Published in 2008 by
Thomson Reuters (Professional) Ireland Limited
(Registered in Ireland, Company No. 80867. Registered Office
and address for service 43 Fitzwilliam Place, Dublin 2)
trading as Round Hall.

Typeset by
Carrigboy Typesetting Services

Reprinted in 2013 by CPI Group (UK) Ltd, Croydon, CR0 4YY

ISBN 978–1–85800–498–3

A catalogue record for this book is available from the British Library.

TABLE OF CONTENTS

PREFACE TO THE SECOND EDITION

Studying the Constitution of Ireland can be a daunting task. Few areas of law have generated so large a body of case law in such a short space of time. Since the publication of the first edition of this Nutshell in 2002 the pace of development has continued unabated, with many important decisions emerging in a variety of key areas. As a result, many students may be put off constitutional law by reason of its sheer size and scope.

This nutshell (as the name suggests) seeks to present constitutional law in a manner that is accessible, informative and succinct. Designed primarily with the busy student in mind, it aims to explain the key principles and concepts of the subject, as well as the major decisions on constitutional matters, in an easily comprehensible way. The Nutshell is framed with particular regard to students who seek a straightforward introduction to constitutional law, as well as those revising for exams.

Given the nature and sheer scope of the subject matter, this text focuses on the key principles of constitutional law, highlighting the most significant and helpful examples of constitutional jurisprudence. As such, it does not purport to be an all-encompassing, exhaustive review of the subject, which is both expansive and highly nuanced. Nonetheless, it is hoped that students will find this introduction useful in their study of constitutional law, providing a sound basis for the further study of cases and commentaries, and clarifying the fundamental principles of law in this area.

In completing this text, and its predecessor, the author is greatly indebted to a number of people. Sincere thanks are due especially to Thérèse Carrick, Dave Ellis and Elina Talvitie in respect of their work on the first edition, and to Susan Rossney, Kristiina Kojamo, Catherine Dolan and Frieda Donohue at Thomson Round Hall for their help and patience in relation to this, the second edition. I take sole responsibility, of course, for all errors made and opinions expressed herein. As always, my sincere gratitude goes to my family and to Chris Roufs, and to my colleagues at D.I.T., especially Bruce Carolan, for their support and patience while the current edition was being completed.

Fergus Ryan
Dublin, April 2008

ADDENDUM:

I have endeavoured to state the law as accurately as I can as of April 30, 2008. Students should, however, bear in mind that constitutional law is constantly evolving.

The Lisbon Treaty of 2007 proposes certain reforms to the institutional structures, law and competences of the European Union. In March 2008 the Government proposed a Twenty-eighth Amendment to the Constitution, which it plans to put to the People in June 2008. If passed, this amendment will allow the ratification of the Treaty. Some changes to the numbering of Art.29 will also occur if the amendment succeeds: in particular Art.29.4.10 (discussed in Ch.6) will become **Article 29.4.9.**

TABLE OF CASES

IRELAND

OTHER

TABLE OF LEGISLATION

CONSTITUTIONAL PROVISIONS

IRISH STATUTES

IRISH STATUTORY INSTRUMENTS

IRISH BILLS

UK LEGISLATION

EUROPEAN UNION LEGISLATION

OTHER

1. INTRODUCTION

The purpose of a constitution

A constitution sets out the basic rules for the running of a state. It typically consists of a series of principles and rules requiring that the affairs of a state be conducted in a particular manner. Ordinarily, it seeks to lay down a framework for the governance of a territory by establishing a set of institutions with responsibility for certain assigned tasks.

A typical constitution broadly sets out to do three things:

1. To determine the boundaries of the State ✶

A constitution often identifies the geographical territory over which state will have power and the extent of that power over the territory. In Ireland's case, Arts 2, 3 and 29.8 of the Irish Constitution establish that while Irish law can have "extra-territorial effect" outside the jurisdiction (allowing it to apply, in special cases, outside of Ireland), it normally applies only to the 26 counties of the State. This means that the institutions of the Irish State ordinarily have power only in respect of what happens within the State as defined.

2. To establish the institutions of the State and to set out the manner in which the State's powers will be distributed between those institutions ✶

In Ireland's case, Arts 12–37 set up a variety of offices and institutions amongst which the powers of the State are divided. The Constitution thus requires the creation of a parliament (the Oireachtas), the lower house of which elects a government (the Executive). It provides for the election of a head of state, the President, and a system of courts, presided over by judges. Each of these functionaries and institutions is allocated certain exclusive tasks. Only the functionary or institution to which a particular task is assigned may perform that function. Furthermore, these tasks may only be performed in compliance with the Constitution.

3. *To regulate the relationship between the State and those resident therein, in particular by securing certain human rights to those residents* ✄

The Irish Constitution is careful to limit the power of the State in certain respects. Thus, in Art.38 and Arts 40–44, the Constitution outlines a series of fundamental rights and freedoms to be enjoyed by citizens and other residents of the State. This effectively precludes the State from acting in contravention of these rights and freedoms.

The Irish Constitution 1937

Although a constitution need not be written, most constitutions are contained in a single document. In Ireland's case this document is Bunreacht na hÉireann or the Constitution of Ireland 1937. The main architect of this Constitution was Éamon de Valera, one of the few surviving leaders of the 1916 Rising, and a leading figure in the Irish War of Independence. With the support of his Fianna Fáil party, he came to power as Prime Minister of the Irish Free State ("President of the Executive Council") in 1932. His purpose in drawing up the 1937 Constitution was largely political. De Valera wanted finally to tear up the Constitution of 1922 and the Anglo–Irish Treaty of 1921 on which it was based. He objected, in particular, to the role that the King of England had under that Treaty and to the partition of Ireland effected thereby. He wanted a United Ireland, North and South, fully independent from the United Kingdom, at least in its internal affairs. Thus the Constitution, as initially drawn up in 1937, contained a legal claim over the territory of Northern Ireland (Arts 2 and 3—see Ch.4 below), though this has since been removed.

Yet despite this revolutionary zeal, de Valera was essentially a conservative man: an intellectual certainly, but also a devout Roman Catholic with a particular view of the way Ireland should progress. The Constitution largely reflects this religious conservatism, in particular in the Preamble, which invokes the "Name of the Most Holy Trinity" and speaks, further, of "all our obligations to our Divine Lord, Jesus Christ". Indeed, as originally conceived, the Constitution included a clause acknowledging the "special position" of the Roman Catholic Church and a ban on divorce, both which clauses have since been removed.

Indicative of the dangerous times in which it was drafted, the Constitution also reflects a concern to preserve and nurture democratic values and the protection of human rights. The role of the President, for instance, is significantly limited (the concern being to prevent facilitating dictatorship), while the right of constitutional amendment was generally reserved to the People alone. The power of judicial review—allowing judges to strike down unconstitutional legislation—is also expressly confirmed.

A dynamic document

Some claim that the Constitution, a creature of its time, is outdated and archaic. In fairness, despite coming into force in 1937, the Constitution has tracked at least some of the social and political changes that have occurred in Ireland in the intervening period. Notably, it has been amended on no less than 23 separate occasions, twice by the Legislature (1939 and 1941) and 21 times by referendum approved by the People. (See Ch.23 below). The contentious legal claim over Northern Ireland, in Arts 2 and 3, for instance, has been dropped (by referendum) in the context of the Good Friday Agreements. (See Ch.4 below). The special position of the Roman Catholic Church and the ban on divorce have met a similar fate at the hands of the People in referendum.

The courts have also acknowledged that even without a referendum, the Constitution is capable of changing with the times. It is, they say, a dynamic document that must be interpreted (read) in the light of prevailing ideas of what is consistent with the common good. A good example is provided by *McGee v Attorney General* [1974] I.R. 284. That case concerned the constitutional validity of legislation banning the sale and importation of artificial contraception. This legislation, notably, had been passed with universal approval in 1935, a mere two years before the Constitution was enacted. Although such a law would more than likely have been deemed constitutional had such a question arisen in 1937, the Supreme Court concluded nonetheless that its hands could not be tied by the views of previous generations. In ruling that the legislation breached the constitutional rights of the plaintiff, the court noted that the Constitution had to be read in a dynamic manner. Otherwise it would become defunct, a code of conduct "frozen in time", irrelevant to the people to whom it was being applied.

2. CONSTITUTIONAL INTERPRETATION

The interpretation or "construction" of the Constitution is a process best described as a search for the true meaning of the Constitution. The role of interpreting the Constitution falls exclusively to the judiciary; the determination of the correct meaning of the text is a matter, in the final analysis, for the courts. There is, however, no single definitive method of interpreting the Constitution, the courts having adopted several different approaches to the issue.

Language

The Constitution is published and promulgated in not one but two languages, Irish and English. Both texts are official texts of the Constitution and a court may proceed by reference to either. In cases of conflict between the two texts, however, the Irish text prevails. In other words, where the Irish and English texts differ in meaning, it is the meaning in the Irish text that is to be preferred (Art.25.5.4°).

Rules of precedent and the doctrine of stare decisis

Before proceeding to the rules of constitutional interpretation, it is necessary to broach the issue of "precedent" in the constitutional context. One of the basic tenets of the common law is that in deciding cases judges must follow "precedent", that is relevant decisions in prior cases. The rule of stare decisis generally demands that judges follow precedent *even if they do not agree with the previous decision*. Precedent demands, in particular, that a lower court always obey the decisions of a higher court, e.g. the High Court always follows the Supreme Court.

These precedent cases also generally bind a court of similar jurisdiction in subsequent cases with the result that the court generally cannot depart from a preceding decision unless:

- the precedent can be distinguished from the case presently before the judge, i.e. because the facts are substantially different from those of the precedent;
- the law has been changed (by legislation or constitutional amendment) since the precedent; or

• justice overwhelmingly demands that the precedent be departed from. This can only be done, however, where the court that set the precedent is a court of "corresponding jurisdiction" (i.e. with the same powers as the court seeking to overturn the precedent). A lower court, of course, can *never* overturn a verdict of a higher court on this ground.

Needless to say, a higher court can always overrule a precedent set by a lower court.

Precedent and the Constitution

The Constitution is said to be a dynamic document capable of changing with the times (see *McGee v Attorney General* [1974] I.R. 284 and *State (Healy) v Donoghue* [1976] I.R. 325). As such, the rules of precedent in the context of constitutional law are subject to the distinct prospect that the interpretation of the Constitution may change from time to time in line with prevailing conceptions of "prudence, justice and charity." In *State (Quinn) v Ryan* [1965] I.R. 70, for instance, the Supreme Court ruled definitively that it is entitled, in appropriate cases, to overrule its own prior decisions on constitutional matters.

Methods of interpretation

The courts have adopted a variety of methods of interpretation, sometimes conflicting, to determine the meaning of constitutional provisions.

Literal interpretation

Adopting a "literal interpretation" of the Constitution presupposes that the words of the Constitution will be given their plain or basic meaning. A literal interpretation thus requires that the straightforward meaning of the words will prevail.

For instance, in *People (DPP) v O'Shea* [1982] I.R. 384, the Supreme Court had to consider whether an appeal could be taken where the High Court had acquitted a suspect of criminal charges. Although the common law rule against double jeopardy prevented an acquittal from being appealed to a higher court, the Supreme Court concluded that the literal meaning of Art.34.4.3° prevailed over this rule. That Article allows all decisions of the High Court to be appealed to the Supreme Court, subject to this right being qualified by legislation (which, in this case, had not occurred). Although the double jeopardy rule is well established and well respected in common law, the Supreme Court nonetheless concluded that it could not argue with the plain meaning of Art.34.

Broad/purposive interpretation

A broad or purposive approach to constitutional interpretation, by contrast, requires that the Constitution be read in the light of its overall purpose or aims. Here it is the spirit rather than the letter of the law that counts. The precise words that are used are not nearly as important as the broad sentiment underlying the Article. Indeed, because the Constitution is a general and sometimes vague document it is often more appropriate to forego a very close parsing of the words in favour of a broader approach to its meaning. It is also worth remembering that the Constitution is a political as well as a legal document.

As Keane C.J. observed in *Maguire v Ardagh* [2002] 2 I.R. 385: "The Constitution is a political charter, using the adjective in its broadest sense. One does not expect to find in it the level of detail which, in our legislative tradition, we associate with Acts, regulations and by-laws."

Example: In *Attorney General v Paperlink* [1984] I.L.R.M. 373 Costello J. rejected an argument that certain semantic differences between Art.40.3.1° and Art.40.3.2°, both of which relate to the various personal rights of citizens, meant that the level of protection afforded by each was different. Article 40.3.1°, for instance, refers to the "respect", "defence" and "vindication" of such rights, whereas Art.40.3.2° speaks only of their "protection" and "vindication". Costello J. nonetheless ruled that these various words offered similar levels of protection for the personal rights covered by each subsection. It was important to consider, he observed, that the Constitution is a political as well as a legal document, and thus contains many relatively broad statements of a general, rhetorical nature. Thus, the Constitution, he concluded, should not be read too literally.

Example: In *O'Byrne v Minister for Finance* [1959] I.R. 1, the Supreme Court had to consider the requirement in Art.35.5 that a judge's remuneration "shall not be reduced" during his tenure in office. The plaintiff, who was the widow of a deceased judge, claimed that the taxation of her husband's salary while he was alive breached this requirement. While it might have been argued, on a literal basis, that the imposition of tax "reduces" one's take-home pay, the Supreme Court adopted a more purposive interpretation. It concluded that the purpose of Art.35.5 was to protect the independence of the judiciary, in particular to prevent the State from attempting to influence a judge's behaviour by threatening to cut his or her salary. The imposition of tax not being, in any real sense, an attack on judicial independence, the court ruled that Art.35.5 had not been breached.

Example: The decision in *M.R. v T.R.* [2006] I.E.H.C. 359 illustrates the use of the purposive approach in the interpretation of constitutional amendments. The Eighth Amendment to the Constitution (passed in 1983) purports to protect the right to life of the unborn child. In this case, McGovern J. looked to the context in which the Eighth Amendment was passed in determining whether the term "unborn child" included an embryo created outside the womb and not yet implanted therein. In concluding that it did not, the learned judge looked to the purpose to which the Amendment was primarily directed: the prevention of abortion. As the central objective of the Amendment was to prevent pregnant women from terminating their pregnancies, the term "unborn child" was read as being restricted to an embryo only *after* it is implanted in the womb and not before.

Harmonious interpretation

The harmonious method of interpretation underlines the point that different parts of the Constitution should not be read in isolation from each other. Instead, they should be read as a set of complementary principles that fall to be interpreted in the light of the whole constitutional document.

For instance, in *Tormey v Ireland* [1985] I.R. 289, the Supreme Court favoured a harmonious interpretation over a literal interpretation of Art.34.3.1, which gives the High Court full original jurisdiction to hear all cases. The plaintiff in this case challenged the constitutionality of legislation transferring jurisdiction in relation to some serious offences from the High Court to the Circuit Court. While the Supreme Court agreed that, on a literal reading, the High Court did enjoy original jurisdiction, it concluded that the Constitution, per Henchy J.:

> "... must be read as a whole ... its several provisions must not
> be looked at in isolation, but treated as interlocking parts of
> the general constitutional scheme."

Thus, where it was possible, reading the Constitution as a whole, to take two different meanings of a provision, the interpretation favouring "the smooth and harmonious operation of the Constitution" should be preferred. In this case, the court noted that the Constitution in several places limits the role of the High Court (e.g. in Art.26 references) and allows other courts (such as the Special Criminal Court and military courts) special powers that effectively oust the High Court's jurisdiction. Article 34.3.4, moreover, allows for the setting up of courts of local and limited jurisdiction, a statement that implied, the court ruled, that the Constitution did not require that all cases be heard at first instance in the High Court.

The courts have frequently suggested that measures permitted by one section of the Constitution may correspondingly be justified generally for the purpose of other sections of the Constitution. For instance, in *Dreher v Irish Land Commission* [1984] I.L.R.M. 94 the Supreme Court noted that a measure found to be justified by Art.43 (protecting the general right to property), cannot simultaneously be deemed an 'unjust attack' on individual property rights under Art.40.3. Similarly, in *Dillane v Ireland* [1980] I.L.R.M. 167 the Supreme Court considered a measure preventing an accused person (found not guilty at trial) recouping his costs from a Garda who took a prosecution against him, in circumstances where a private person taking such a prosecution would not have been so exempted. The Supreme Court reasoned that the special treatment of Gardaí in this instance was justified under Art.40.1 (which generally requires equal treatment before the law) as Gardaí held a different social function to lay litigants (see below at p.127). Having so concluded, the court declined to rule that the special treatment of Gardaí constituted an unjust attack on the plaintiff's property rights contrary to Art.40.3. As the difference of treatment was "... categorically permitted by Article 40.1, so it cannot be part of the injustice which Article 40.3.2 was designed to prevent". The courts have also noted (e.g. in *Irish Times v Ireland* [1998] 1 I.R. 359) that the duty to administer justice in public must be read as being qualified by the rights of the accused under Art.38.1, such that media reporting of court proceedings can be curtailed where necessary to ensure the accused's right to a fair trial even if this is not required by legislation. This is despite an express requirement in Art.34.1 that all cases should be heard in public unless otherwise required by legislation.

A case that lies on the borders of harmonious interpretation is *O'B. v S.* [1984] I.R. 316. There, the Supreme Court decided that discrimination against the children of unmarried parents was justified by the constitutional preference for marriage in Art.41. The plaintiff's father had died intestate (without making a will). However, as her parents had not been married to each other, she was not (at that time) entitled to a share in his estate. Had her parents been married to each other, by contrast, she would have been entitled to succeed to his property. This, the court agreed, was discrimination that would ordinarily have infringed Art.40.1, the guarantee of equality. Nonetheless, Art.40.1, the judges said, had to be read in the light of the constitutional preference for marriage contained in Art.41. This, they concluded, justified the discrimination of which she complained. (The Status of Children Act 1987 subsequently removed this discriminatory provision.)

On one view, this case illustrates a tendency to read the different parts of the Constitution as a coherent whole, the policy of one article being reflected by the others. Yet *O'B.* suggests that, in fact, certain articles of the Constitution take precedence over others. To some extent in every case of harmonious interpretation a value judgment arises that favours certain constitutional principles over others, a point discussed further below.

Hierarchical interpretation

The hierarchical method of interpretation presupposes that some constitutional values are more important than others. While there is no definitive list prioritising certain rights, some clearly rank higher than others. Thus where there exists a straightforward conflict between the terms of one right and those of another, or between the respective rights of two individuals, the court may decide that one right takes priority over the other. The best example is the right to life, which has virtually consistently "trumped" (won out over) lesser rights in the constitutional scheme.

Example: One controversial example of this concerns the right to life of the unborn. In the *Attorney General v Open Door Counselling* [1988] I.R. 593, the Supreme Court ruled that the unborn's right to life took precedence over any right to distribute information that facilitated a woman wishing to obtain an abortion in the UK. While the Fourteenth Amendment to the Constitution 1992 subsequently conferred an express right to information of this nature, a separate controversy still surrounds the balance between the right to life of the unborn and the equal right to life accorded to its mother. In *Attorney General v X.* [1992] 1 I.R. 1, the Supreme Court agreed that the mother's life took precedence over the child's in cases where there was a real and substantial risk to the life of the mother.

Example: A less controversial example is afforded by the *People (DPP) v Shaw* [1982] I.R. 1. In that case a person suspected of kidnapping a woman had been arrested. He was, however, illegally detained *beyond* the time at which he should either have been charged or released. The Supreme Court nonetheless found that this illegal detention was constitutionally excused on the ground that the Gardaí had acted with a view to saving the life of the kidnapped woman. Although the woman in question was not found alive, the court ruled that the Gardaí's concern to vindicate the right to life of the woman justified the breach of the defendant's right to liberty. Similarly in *Foley v Sunday Newspapers Ltd* [2005] 1 I.R. 89, Kelly J. noted that however important freedom of the press might be, it cannot equal or exceed the protection afforded to the right to life. Thus if there was sufficiently compelling evidence that media coverage of a trial would endanger the life of any person, the court would restrict such coverage. *Foley* illustrates, however, that it is not enough simply to assert the superior right—the risk to life must be established.

The hierarchies of the Constitution are not always easily explained. In the context of elections, the courts have ruled, for instance, that the individual right to vote is less important than the integrity of the election process generally (see *Draper v Attorney General* [1984] I.R. 277). By contrast, the requirement of a secret ballot was favoured over the integrity of the voting system in *McMahon v Attorney General* [1972] I.R. 69. Similarly the courts have generally subordinated the requirement of non-discrimination on religious grounds in favour of supporting the free practice of religion as a superior right, both being guaranteed by Art.44. As we saw in *O'B. v S.* the protection of marriage ranks above the principle of equality, even where children are involved. While such conclusions may be justified, it arguably involves the courts in making value judgments about the relative importance of constitutional principles. Who is to say, for instance, that in *O'B. v S.* the protection of the institution of marriage qualifies the guarantee of equality? Could the courts not just as easily have concluded that the marriage clause was subject to an overriding requirement of equal treatment, at least in relation to children?

Historical interpretation

The courts very often look to the state of the law or public opinion at the time that the Constitution was enacted as a guide to its meaning. In particular, if a specific practice was commonplace before 1937, but was not expressly prohibited by the Constitution, it might be reasonable to assume that it was intended to continue that practice. On the other hand, where something expressly provided for in the Constitution of 1922 or preceding law is not expressly provided for in the current Constitution, an inference may be drawn that it was not intended to be allowed.

There follow some examples of cases in which the historical approach has been accepted. In *Conroy v Attorney General* [1965] I.R. 411, the Supreme Court had to consider whether an offence was or was not a "minor" offence: an offence that could be tried without a jury (see below at pp.122–124). In deciding that it was a "minor offence", the court took into account the fact that at the time of enactment of the Constitution the relevant offence was treated as minor in nature. Similarly, in *Melling v Ó Mathghamhna* [1962] I.R. 1, the Supreme Court looked to the state of law in 1937 in determining the intended scope of the words "minor offence".

In *Norris v Attorney General* [1984] I.R. 36, O'Higgins C.J. suggested that the historical Christian prejudice against homosexuality justified his conclusion that there was no constitutional right to engage in homosexual sexual activity. The courts have also referred to 19th and 20th century developments in education in the *Campaign to Separate Church and State v Ireland* in interpreting the "endowment" of religion prohibited by Art.44. Similarly, in *Maguire v Ardagh* [2002] 1 I.R. 385, the Supreme Court had regard to the historical context in which the 1922 and 1937 Constitutions were enacted in determining the scope of the power of the Oireachtas to establish investigative committees.

The courts have also looked to the historical and political context in which constitutional amendments have been passed to elicit the meaning of certain provisions of the Constitution enacted after 1937. For instance in *M.R. v T.R.* [2006] I.E.H.C. 359 the High Court looked to the political context in which the Eighth Amendment to the Constitution was passed in 1983 to determine the meaning of "unborn child" as used in Art.40.3.3. Looking to the historical context in which the referendum was proposed—the primary concern being to restrict the termination of pregnancies (abortion)—McGovern J. concluded that the term "unborn child" meant only an embryo within the womb and not an embryo not yet implanted in the womb.

Is an updating construction (interpretation) permitted? There is clearly some logic, in determining the meaning of the Constitution, in enquiring into the intention of the drafters and the historical context in which the Constitution was passed. Nevertheless, this tendency must be used cautiously. The danger otherwise arises that the Constitution will become frozen in time, framed by reference to an era very different from our own. On several occasions the courts have noted that the Constitution is a "dynamic" document, capable of changing with the times (see per O'Higgins C.J. in *State (Healy) v Donoghue* [1976] I.R. 325). In *McGee v Attorney General* [1974] I.R. 284, for instance, the Supreme Court ruled that a ban on the importation of contraception infringed the constitutional right to marital privacy. This was despite the fact that this ban was introduced only two years before the Constitution was enacted and with apparently universal public and legislative support.

On the other hand, the facility allowing the Constitution to change with the times presents a uniquely difficult challenge to judges—how do judges tell that attitudes have changed sufficiently to allow for a changed interpretation of the Constitution? In *Zappone and Gilligan v Revenue Commissioners* [2006] I.E.H.C. 404 Dunne J., while agreeing that the meaning of the Constitution was capable of alteration in line with changed times and attitudes, observed that this could only be done where there was sufficient evidence of a consensus for change. At the time the Constitution was enacted, the term 'marriage' as used in Art.41 clearly denoted, she believed, a heterosexual marriage. While this understanding was capable of evolving over time, the judge concluded that there was not sufficient evidence of a consensus for change. She pointed in particular to the fact that legislation banning same-sex marriage (the Civil Registration Act 2004) was passed only two years before her judgment.

The natural rights approach

The Constitution is sometimes read, particularly where the court seeks to establish certain rights, by reference to what is called "natural law".

Natural law is said to be a type of universal law that exists independently of "positive" or "man-made" law. Natural law is considered, moreover, to be a species of "divine reason", God's plan for the universe revealed to us through the use of human reason. It is said that we as humans can determine certain universal truths or "laws" through the use of reason, in particular by observing nature and learning from the natural order of things.

Some, like the great philosopher and jurist Jeremy Bentham, considered such theories to be "nonsense on stilts". It is not easy to disagree, moreover, with those who suggest that natural law reasoning can be used to support whatever conclusion a judge considers appropriate in a given case. That said, natural law reasoning has proved quite popular amongst Irish judges. These judges have regularly acknowledged that the Irish Constitution protects rights that are not created by the Constitution itself but which "inhere in the individual" as "natural rights".

For instance, in *McGee v Attorney General* [1974] I.R. 284, Walsh J. observed that the Constitution in Arts 41, 42 and 43 alike expressly refers to certain rights and duties as being "natural" and, moreover, as existing independently of any man-made law. These rights are, furthermore, said to be "antecedent [prior to] and superior" to human laws. The Constitution nonetheless protects such rights as universal human rights, notwithstanding the fact that at least some of these rights are not even mentioned in the Constitution.

It is worth noting however, that the natural rights approach cannot be used to frustrate the will of the people clearly expressed in a referendum. In the Art.26 reference of the *Regulation of Information Bill 1995* [1995] 1 I.R. 1 the Supreme Court rejected the contention that an Amendment to the Constitution that infringed the natural law would be unenforceable. The sovereignty (supreme power) of the People in referendum permits them, the court reasoned, to amend the Constitution in any way they wish. Even if such amendment infringed natural law it would nonetheless be constitutionally sound. (For a further exposition of this issue see below at p.189)

The presumption of constitutionality

In law, one is often permitted to "presume" certain things, until the contrary is proved. For instance, an accused person is presumed innocent until his or her guilt is proved beyond a reasonable doubt (see below at pp.113–114). This is also called the "onus" or "burden" of proof. Similarly, where a law is created by the Oireachtas it is generally presumed, until the contrary is proved, that the legislation is constitutional. The burden of proving that the legislation is unconstitutional, in other words, is upon the person who makes this allegation.

> Article 15.4 states that the Oireachtas shall not enact laws that are contrary to the Constitution. Because of the respect that each institution of State has for the others, the courts must not assume too readily that the Oireachtas has acted in contravention of the Constitution.

That said, the presumption of constitutionality *does not* prevent a law from being found unconstitutional. It simply makes it harder to prove such an allegation.

- In some cases the breach of the Constitution will be so obvious that the presumption will be rendered especially weak. In *M. v An Bord Uchtála* [1977] I.R. 287, for instance, a provision that prevented couples of mixed religion from adopting children was struck down. This measure being so very obviously contrary to the freedom of religion (and implicitly perhaps, to the right to marry), Pringle J. felt that the presumption was especially weak in this case.
- Analogous principles apply where a piece of legislation contains a provision that is substantially similar or identical to one previously deemed unconstitutional by the courts. In *Re Article 26 and the Equal Status Bill 1997* [1997] 2 I.R. 387, the Supreme Court declined to apply the presumption of constitutionality to a measure that was identical in substance to a provision of the Employment Equality Bill 1996 which had earlier been found to be unconstitutional. (*Re Article 26 and the Employment Equality Bill 1996* [1997] 2 I.R. 321.)
- The presumption does not apply to Acts passed before 1937. Logically, one cannot presume that a piece of legislation passed before the Constitution was enacted was created with the Constitution's terms in mind. See, for example, *McGee v Attorney General* [1974] I.R. 284, where the Supreme Court ruled that the presumption of constitutionality did not apply to an Act of Parliament passed in 1935. By the same token, Acts passed by the British Parliament before 1922 cannot be presumed to have been enacted in compliance with the Irish Constitution.

- The presumption does, however, apply to Bills passed by the Oireachtas and referred to the Supreme Court under Art.26, even though such Bills are not yet "law". Although it is not yet an enforceable "law", one must assume that the Houses of the Oireachtas would not intentionally have passed unconstitutional legislation. (See below at pp.17–21)

- As a corollary to the presumption, where a body or person is given a power or discretion under law, it must be assumed that that body or person is required to exercise that power or discretion in compliance with the Constitution (see *East Donegal Co-operative v Attorney General* [1970] I.R. 317).

The double construction rule

Take the situation where there are two or more possible interpretations (meanings) of legislation open to a court, one of which would render the legislation constitutional and the others unconstitutional. In such a case the double construction rule dictates that the interpretation that renders the legislation constitutional is to be preferred.

Example: For instance, in *Re Haughey* [1971] I.R. 217, the Supreme Court had to consider the legality of an Act that allowed a Dáil committee to "certify" that a person had committed a criminal offence. There were two possible interpretations of this clause:

- the Committee was given the power to find the person guilty of an offence (which is unconstitutional—only a court can find someone guilty of a crime); (see below at p.121.)
- the Committee could refer the matter to the High Court, which would then consider the guilt of the accused.

Both interpretations being open to the court, and the first involving an unconstitutional act, the second interpretation was to be preferred.

3. JUDICIAL REVIEW—CHALLENGING THE CONSTITUTIONALITY OF STATE CONDUCT

General remarks

Judicial review is the process by which the courts may declare invalid legislation that is unconstitutional. Where either the High Court or Supreme Court finds that legislation, or any part of such legislation, infringes a provision of the Constitution, it is empowered to declare such unconstitutional provisions to be null and void. This means that the provisions are deemed to be unlawful and of no legal effect.

There are several different procedures for striking down such legislation, each concerning different types of law. These procedures are set out in Arts 34, 50 and 26 respectively.

Article 34

Where legislation or a Government measure was passed after the coming into force of the Constitution, Art.34.3.2° applies. This allows the High Court (and on appeal the Supreme Court) to assess the constitutional validity of any provision of law. Where such a law is found to be unconstitutional, it must be declared to be null and void and of no legal effect (though only to the extent that the measure is unconstitutional).

Where the court is considering a law passed by the Oireachtas after 1937, two provisions apply:

- **the presumption of constitutionality** (see above at pp.13–15);
- **the one judgment rule**: where the Supreme Court is considering such an Act, it may only hand down one judgment, i.e. that of the court. No other judgment, dissenting or otherwise, may be expressed. Even where there is a difference of opinion between judges, it is not open to the court or to any judge thereof to indicate that such a difference of opinion existed (see Art.34.4.5°).

It is important to note that where a section or part of an Act is deemed unconstitutional, only that section or part is null and void, the remainder of the Act retaining its legal force.

Article 50

Special considerations apply to legislation and other measures brought into force before the Constitution was enacted. Such legislation is said to be "carried over" into the laws of the new State subject to two conditions:

* to the extent only that such legislation has not been repealed, i.e. the legislation must have been in force on December 29, 1937; and
* to the extent only that such legislation is not inconsistent with the Constitution.

Where a legislative provision has been repealed prior to the enactment of the Constitution, it cannot be carried over. In a similar vein, where a specific provision is found to be unconstitutional, it is deemed never to have been carried over into the law of the new State. **N.B.** Neither the presumption of constitutionality nor the one judgment rule apply to measures passed before December 29, 1937.

Article 26

A special provision of the Constitution, Art.26, allows the constitutionality of a Bill to be assessed before the President signs the Bill into law.

* **What does Art.26 do?** Article 26 allows the President to refer a Bill (or a part of such a Bill) not yet signed by her to the Supreme Court. The purpose of such a reference is to test whether the Bill, or any specified part of it, is unconstitutional.
* **What is a "Bill" for these purposes?** A Bill, for the purposes of Art.26, is a piece of legislation passed (or deemed to have been passed) by both Houses of the Oireachtas but not yet signed by the President. Certain types of Bill cannot be referred: these include Bills proposing a change to the Constitution, and "Money Bills" (see below at p.80).
* **Can only a part of a Bill be referred?** While most Art.26 cases concern entire Bills, the President is free to refer only a section or part of a Bill, as she sees fit. *Re Article 26 and Section 4 of the School Attendance Bill 1942* [1943] I.R. 334 and *Re Article 26 and Part V of the Planning and Development Act 1999* [2001] 1 I.L.R.M.81, are noteworthy, involving as they did the referral of only a *part* (and not the whole) of a Bill. Yet even if only a part of

a Bill is referred and that part alone is found to be unconstitutional, no part of the Bill may become law.

- **Who may make an Article 26 reference?** The President alone
  may make such a reference. No other person may make an
  Article 26 reference.
- **Does the President act alone in making the reference?** Before
  making a reference, the President must first consult with the
  Council of State, a body that advises the President on the
  performance of her functions. (See below at pp.59–60). While
  she is obliged to seek the Council's prior advice, the President
  may, however, choose to ignore its advice. In the final analysis,
  the question as to whether a Bill should be referred is a matter for
  the President alone to decide.
- **Does the Bill have to be considered by the High Court first?**
  No. The President makes the reference directly to the Supreme
  Court, by-passing all lower courts.
- **How many judges of the Supreme Court must hear such a
  reference?** At least five.
- **Do they hear argument first?** Yes. Counsel is appointed to
  represent the opposing perspectives in the case. The Attorney
  General usually selects two barristers to argue for the validity of
  the Bill. The court will generally appoint a similar number of
  barristers to argue against its validity. It is possible for the court to
  appoint barristers to argue against the Bill from conflicting
  perspectives as in *Re Article 26 and the Regulation of Information
  Bill 1995* [1995] 1 I.R. 1. This Bill concerned the vexed issue of
  information on abortion. Pro-life advocates claimed that the Bill
  endangered the right to life of the unborn child. Pro-choice
  advocates, by contrast, counter-argued that the Bill was so
  restrictive that it infringed a woman's right to be informed about
  the options available on pregnancy. While the Supreme Court
  ultimately found that the Bill was constitutional, *two* groups of
  counsel were appointed to argue against the Bill, one set representing the interests of unborn children, the other set representing
  the perspective of a mother contemplating an abortion.
- **Does the presumption of constitutionality apply to such Bills?**
  Yes. Even though the Bill is not yet "law", it is assumed that
  Parliament did not act contrary to the Constitution in enacting its
  provisions. This presumption can, of course, be rebutted
  (overturned) by evidence showing that the Bill (or part thereof) is

unconstitutional. The only exception arises where a measure in the Bill has already been found to be unconstitutional in a previous case. Thus, notably, in *Re Article 26 and the Equal Status Bill 1996* [1997] 2 I.R. 387, the Supreme Court refused to apply the presumption in circumstances where the Bill replicated provisions that the court had previously found to be unconstitutional in *Re Article 26 and the Employment Equality Bill 1996* [1997] 2 I.R. 387.

The finding of the court

After the court deliberates it makes its decision. Article 26.2.2° allows the court to issue only one judgment, representing the opinion of the whole court. Even if individual judges disagree with the decision, they cannot openly express such dissent.

If **NO** part of the Bill is found to be unconstitutional, the President *must* sign the Bill into law. Once signed by the President, the Bill becomes an Act of Parliament. An Act that is passed after an Art.26 reference may never again be challenged on the grounds that it infringes the Constitution. If only a part of a Bill was being considered by the court, only that part enjoys constitutional immunity after the Bill becomes an Act.

If **ANY** part of the Bill is found to be unconstitutional, however, the President *must not* sign the Bill into law. No part of the Bill can become law, *even* those parts that are found to be constitutional. For example, in *Re Article 26 and the Employment Equality Bill 1996* [1997] 2 I.R. 321, the Supreme Court expressly found that a section purporting to exempt religious organisations from the terms of the Bill was constitutionally valid. Nonetheless, because other parts of the Bill were unconstitutional, no part of the Bill could become law. Similarly, in *Re Article 26 and the Health (Amendment) (No. 2) Bill 2004* [2005] I.E.S.C. 7, the Bill could not be signed into law even though some of its provisions (those that were not retrospective) had expressly been found to be constitutionally valid, because other provisions were unconstitutional.

Notably, it is not possible to sever the offending portions and pass the rest of the Bill into law. The entirety of the Bill either stands or falls. It is also important to note that while Parliament may sometimes introduce a *new* Bill with similar provisions (absent those found to be unconstitutional), the Supreme Court *never* "refers back" legislation to Parliament.

Cases where Bills or parts of Bills have been found to be unconstitutional

In all, various Presidents have referred 15 separate Bills to the Supreme Court, seven of which have been deemed unconstitutional in whole or in part:

• The School Attendance Bill 1942
• The Housing (Private Rented Dwellings) Amendment Bill 1982
• The Electoral (Amendment) Bill 1983
• The Matrimonial Home Bill 1993
• The Employment Equality Bill 1996
• The Equal Status Bill 1997
• The Health (Amendment) (No. 2) Bill 2004

The advantages and disadvantages of the Article 26 procedure

Advantages

• Article 26 allows a Bill to be tested in court before it causes any harm to a member of the public. Thus, problems with the Bill can be identified before the Bill has breached any individual's constitutional rights.
• In some cases, it would not be possible for a person who might be aggrieved by legislation to take a case concerning its provisions. A good example would be the unborn child, who would clearly not be in a position to challenge laws that potentially infringe its rights (see, for instance, the reference of the *Regulation of Information Bill 1995* [1995] 1 I.R. 1). An Art.26 reference would also be useful where the Bill purports to infringe the rights of persons who might not be in a position to afford to sue the State.
• From the State's perspective, it knows that if a Bill passes the Art.26 test, it can never again be challenged in court once it becomes an Act.

Disadvantages

• Only the President may make a reference under Art.26. Other concerned citizens may not do so. Moreover, no one can force the President to take such a case, even if it is quite obvious that a Bill is unconstitutional.

- Article 26 proceedings rely entirely on moot arguments. As there are no "real people" in court claiming that their rights have been breached, the lawyers have to imagine hypothetical scenarios in which the Bill may infringe the rights of an individual. It is not beyond the realms of possibility, thus, that the lawyers involved may, quite reasonably, not envision the full implications of a Bill.
- Where a Bill is found to be constitutional, the legislation may never be challenged again. This remains the case even if it subsequently becomes clear that the law in fact infringes constitutional rights. For instance, in *Re Ó Láighléis* [1960] I.R. 93, the applicant challenged the constitutionality of the Offences Against the State (Amendment) Act 1940, under which he had been imprisoned without trial. Because that Act (while a Bill) had successfully survived an Art.26 reference, it could not be so challenged, regardless of the merits of Mr Ó Láighléis's case.
- The time for judicial consideration of Bills is comparatively short. The court must report to the President within 60 days of the referral. Hence, if the matter under scrutiny proves particularly complex, the court may not have sufficient time to consider it.
- Even if only one short section of a lengthy Bill is found to be unconstitutional, no part of the Bill may become law. The remainder of what might otherwise be a good Bill falls by the wayside just because one article is defective.

Only certain persons may challenge the constitutionality of an Act

Locus standi—the standing of a person to challenge the consti- tutionality of a law

"Locus standi" is a Latin phrase meaning a person's legal "standing" or right to sue. A person is ordinarily said to have locus standi to challenge the constitutionality of State conduct only if he or she has been or stands to be directly and adversely affected by such conduct. The litigant must show that the measure directly and personally affects their interest. For instance, one cannot generally complain that a statute is unconstitutional simply because it infringes the rights of third parties (i.e. people other than the person making the complaint). Take the following situation: John and Jane both believe that a particular Act of Parliament infringes the right to equality by treating women less favourably than men. Only Jane could sue, John not being a person actually adversely affected by such unfavourable treatment.

The leading case in this area is *Cahill v Sutton* [1980] I.R. 269. Here, the Supreme Court ruled that the plaintiff could not invoke in her favour the fact that a law breached the rights of a third party (a *"jus tertii"*). The plaintiff, who had been injured as a result of negligence, lost the right to sue in respect of her injuries, because she had not commenced proceedings within the set time period laid down by the Statute of Limitations 1957. It was alleged that this Act infringed the constitutional rights of those who did not discover their injuries until after the period of limitation had expired. Yet, as the plaintiff herself had known of her injuries long before the period of limitation ran out, she did not have locus standi to make this argument. The court noted, in particular, that in order to challenge a legal rule one must show that the law adversely affected or endangered the personal interests of the party challenging the rule.

Thus, in *Norris v Attorney General* [1984] I.R. 36, the plaintiff was precluded from alleging that a legislative ban on "buggery" (anal intercourse) infringed the rights of married persons, as the plaintiff was not himself a married person.

The relaxation of the rule of locus standi

The rule of locus standi in constitutional cases has, however, been relaxed to allow constitutional challenges to proceed even where the parties cannot show that they are directly and personally affected by a breach of the Constitution. Where a measure potentially affects the public at large, rather than one specific person or group of people, the litigant can nonetheless take a case even though she cannot differentiate herself from other citizens:

*   **The "bona fide" interest group**. A body of persons may plead a breach of the Constitution where that organisation has a genuine concern in seeing that the terms of the Constitution are upheld. In *S.P.U.C. v Coogan* [1989] I.R. 734, for instance, the Supreme Court allowed a group interested in protecting the lives of the unborn to plead that the defendants had endangered those lives. This was despite the clear fact that none of the plaintiffs were themselves unborn children.

- **The "actio popularis"**. A person may also take a case where it affects the interests and rights of the public as a whole although no one person stands individually to be affected more than another person. For instance, in *Crotty v An Taoiseach* [1987] I.R. 713, the Supreme Court allowed a concerned citizen to plead that the terms of the Single European Act undermined the exclusive right of the State to determine its own foreign policy. This was despite the fact that Mr Crotty was no more likely to suffer under the Treaty than any other member of the population. Likewise in *Martin v Dublin Corporation* unreported, High Court, November 14, 1978, a historian was permitted to challenge a plan to build offices over the site of the remains of a Viking settlement at Wood Quay, Dublin. Although ultimately unsuccessful, the court allowed the case to proceed, notwithstanding the fact that this was not a matter of personal grievance but one potentially affecting the people of Dublin generally.
- Restrictions may, however, be placed on locus standi with a view to protecting the courts from what is seen as an abuse of the judicial process or from frivolous or vexatious claims (claims without foundation or designed primarily to stir up trouble). In *Riordan v Ireland (No. 4)* [2001] 3 I.R. 365 the Supreme Court placed restrictions on a litigant with a long history of taking cases in what he believed to be the public interest, preventing him from mounting further challenges without first obtaining the leave of the court. While the plaintiff had a right to litigate, this was not an absolute right: it was one that had, in particular, to be balanced against other citizens' right to be protected from "unnecessary harassment and expense". See also *Riordan v An Taoiseach* (No. 5) [2001] 4 I.R. 463 and *Riordan v An Taoiseach* [2006] I.E.H.C. 312.

Certain provisions can never be the subject of judicial review

Emergency powers—Article 28.3

Legislation passed under the provisions of Art.28.3 cannot be challenged in respect of its constitutionality, even if such legislation clearly infringes the Constitution. Article 28.3 applies to specified legislation enacted in times of war, armed rebellion or other conflict. Such times of war or armed rebellion may include situations in which the State is not directly a participant, for example the Second World

War (where Ireland was technically neutral) and the former "Troubles" in Northern Ireland.

Article 28.3 applies to three different scenarios.

- Where the State is a participant in a war or an armed rebellion. In such cases legislation "expressed to be for the purpose of securing the public safety and the preservation of the State in time of war or armed rebellion" cannot be found unconstitutional.
- Where there is an armed conflict in which the State is not a participant. In such cases a declaration must be passed by both Houses of the Oireachtas to the effect that "a national emergency exists affecting the vital interests of the State". Again, such legislation will only be immune from constitutional challenge where it is "expressed to be for the purpose of securing the public safety and the preservation of the State in time of war or armed rebellion".
- After the termination of such war, conflict or armed rebellion, a state of emergency will continue in force until each House of the Oireachtas passes a resolution to the effect that the situation of peril has ceased to exist.

The application of Article 28.3. In September 1939 Germany invaded Poland, precipitating the Second World War. Although Ireland declared itself neutral in this matter, both Houses of the Oireachtas resolved that a national emergency existed such that certain legislation passed by those Houses would be beyond legal challenge. This state of emergency was not officially terminated until 1976, when a new set of resolutions was passed in respect of the Northern Ireland Troubles. This new state of emergency, in turn, only ended in 1995.

Notably, not every piece of legislation passed during an emergency is constitutionally immune. In fact, it is quite rare for legislation to be passed invoking Art.28.3. To qualify for the exemption under Art.28.3, the legislation in question must expressly invoke that Article. One such piece of legislation was the Emergency Powers Act 1976. This legislation concerned certain powers of arrest that were alleged to have been unconstitutional. This provision, before it became an Act, was the subject of an Art.26 reference (*Re the Emergency Powers Bill 1975* [1977] I.R. 129). In the course of its judgment, the Supreme Court made the following points:

- Acts passed under Art.28.3 cannot be challenged on the basis of the unconstitutionality of their substantive content;
- The courts may, however, check that any legislation passed under Art.28.3 complied with the *procedures* for the adoption of such legislation as laid out in that Article;
- Even though the Constitution cannot be invoked to strike down such legislation, it is not to be assumed too readily that the legislation was enacted in breach of the Constitution. For instance, while the Emergency Powers Bill purported to allow a person to be detained for seven days without charge, the court found that such people still enjoyed certain constitutional rights, including the right to a lawyer, the right to medical treatment and the right not to be oppressively interrogated.

N.B. Article 15.5.2 precludes the State from using Art.28.3 to impose a death penalty, even in times of emergency.

European Union law

Measures passed by the institutions of the European Union are exempted by Art.29.4.10 from constitutional scrutiny. This means that legislation adopted by the EU can become part of Irish law without having to comply with the Constitution. Article 29.4.10, moreover, exempts from constitutional scrutiny any measure adopted by the State that is "necessitated by the obligations of membership" of the Union. The meaning of this phrase and the implications of Art.29.4.10° generally are examined further below in Ch.6.

Other miscellaneous matters

Other miscellaneous matters remain outside the scope of review of the courts.

- The decision of the Director of Public Prosecutions (DPP) to prosecute or not to prosecute a person in respect of a crime can only be challenged in court where it can be shown that the DPP has acted in bad faith or with an improper motive (see *State (McCormack) v Curran* [1987] I.L.R.M. 225). Similar provisions apply to the DPP's decision to refer an accused person's case to the Special Criminal Court (see *Savage v DPP* [1982] I.L.R.M. 385).

- The decision of the Government to establish a Special Criminal Court under the provisions of the Offences Against the State Act 1939 is not subject to judicial review (see *Kavanagh v Ireland* [1996] 1 I.R. 321).
- The President is not answerable to the courts or the Oireachtas in respect of the performance of her functions. (Art.13.8)
- As a result of Art.15.10, the internal operations of the Houses of the Oireachtas are not amenable to court review. Likewise members of Parliament are not amenable to the courts for statements made in either House. (Arts 15.12 and 15.13).

The effects of a finding of unconstitutionality

It is well established that where a court finds that a piece of legislation is unconstitutional, that provision is said to be null and void and of no legal effect. It is said, moreover, that such unconstitutional legislation *never* at any time had the force of law. In other words, the legislation is said to be illegal with "retrospective" effect.

In recent years, however, the full force and logic of this view has been substantially challenged and qualified. Indeed in practice the courts have always found ways to limit the consequences of a finding of unconstitutionality. There are now significant limits on the extent to which a person can claim retrospective relief where a statute is found to be unconstitutional. In particular, the decision in *A. v Governor of Arbour Hill Prison* [2006] I.E.S.C. 45, discussed below at pp.28–29, has greatly restricted the effects of a finding of unconstitutionality. The reasoning in this and other cases appears to be based on pragmatic grounds, the key concern being the need to maintain order and the observance of the law.

The classical view

The classical view is that everything done under an unconstitutional law is also deemed to be legally ineffective. For instance, if an Act was passed in 1968 and found to be unconstitutional by a court in 2000, the view is taken that the Act is deemed to have been illegal not only from the date of the judgment but also from its very inception in 1968. This means that anything done under the legislation is deemed in theory to have been illegally done, again with retrospective effect.

Murphy v Attorney General: limits on the right to recoup overpaid taxes

In *Murphy v Attorney General* [1982] I.R. 241, the Supreme Court examined the retrospective effect of a finding of unconstitutionality. In that case, the Supreme Court struck down provisions of the tax code that potentially taxed married couples more than unmarried couples with similar living arrangements. This, the court found, constituted an unjust attack on the institution of marriage contrary to Art.41.

The next question that arose in this context was whether and to what extent married couples were entitled to a refund of all the surplus tax that was unlawfully collected by the State from the date that the Act had been created to the date of the judgment. Potentially, many couples had, over the several decades following the inception of the Constitution, paid more tax than they were constitutionally required to pay. In theory, the court said, these taxes were collected illegally and were thus theoretically refundable. Nevertheless, the court ruled that these surplus taxes would only have to be refunded to those who had already commenced proceedings at the date of the judgment. Even in those cases, the parties would be entitled to reclaim the excess taxes paid only from the date on which they had commenced proceedings against the State.

The reasoning of the court was as follows: the State was entitled to assume, where people had paid their taxes without protest, that the money could be used by the State. The State having spent the money that was collected in good faith, it could not now be ordered to repay that money. Thus, it was only where the taxes had been paid pending legal proceedings that the State could be obliged to repay the surplus monies collected. In making this decision, the court had particular regard to the financial position of the State, which would have been severely compromised had every person who overpaid tax on the basis of the unconstitutional action of the State been entitled to reclaim it. (At the time, the economic situation of the State was quite poor). (See, however, *Muckley v Ireland* [1985] I.R. 782).

The modern view—the rights of prisoners convicted under laws subsequently deemed unconstitutional

Difficult questions arise where a person is convicted of a crime under a law subsequently found to be unconstitutional. Although the law is deemed retrospectively to be null and void and of no legal effect, this does not mean that the conviction will be quashed. The *State (Byrne) v Frawley* [1978] I.R. 326 concerned an accused man who was tried before a jury that had been selected in an unconstitutional manner. Although the accused was aware of this fact at the time of the trial, he chose not to complain about it until *after* he had been convicted. The Supreme Court ruled that as the complainant had not, at the time of his trial, made any objection to the method of jury selection, he had effectively "waived" his right to complain. As the complainant did not assert his right at the time of the trial, he could not subsequently object to the jury that he had accepted. Similarly in *McDonnell v Ireland* [1998] 1 I.R. 134 the Supreme Court refused to compensate a postman who lost his job as a result of a criminal law measure subsequently found to be unconstitutional. The court concluded that the postman had delayed in taking action, and should thus be denied relief. O'Flaherty J., however, expressed the view that "laws must be observed until struck down as unconstitutional". Once an Act is passed, citizens and the State alike were obliged to follow the law. As such, taking into account "the requirements of an ordered society" O'Flaherty J. suggested that the State could not be faulted for following a law that had not yet been found unconstitutional. This was particularly so where the person seeking relief had not sought to challenge the measure before it was found to be invalid.

The most recent decision on this point, and arguably the most important, is *A. v Governor of Arbour Hill Prison* [2006] I.E.S.C. 56. In an earlier case, *C.C. v Ireland (No. 2)* [2006] I.E.S.C. 33, the Supreme Court struck down as unconstitutional part of a 1935 Act banning carnal knowledge of (sexual intercourse with) a girl under the age of 15. As the Act did not afford a defence of genuine mistake as to the alleged victim's age, the Supreme Court concluded that the law infringed the right to liberty under Art.40 of the Constitution. (See below at pp.121–122). In the *A.* case, a man who had been convicted of unlawful carnal knowledge of a 12-year-old girl, claimed the benefit of the decision in *C.C.* As he had been convicted under a provision found to be unconstitutional, he was (he claimed) entitled to be released.

The court agreed that an Act once found unconstitutional is considered null and void from the date of its enactment, or, if it was passed before 1937, the date of the enactment of the Constitution itself. However, in a ruling that greatly limits the impact of a finding of unconstitutionality, the Supreme Court upheld the conviction, refusing to order the release of Mr A. An approach that invalidated all actions taken on foot of a law found subsequently to be unconstitutional would in the words of Murray C.J. "… render the Constitution dysfunctional, and ignore that it contains a complete set of rules and principles designed to ensure an ordered society under the rule of law …".

In particular, the court noted that the State was entitled and was required to observe all laws until such time as they are declared unconstitutional. Neither the State nor individuals are free to disobey a law; officers and institutions of State, moreover, are expected to enforce and uphold the law and can hardly be faulted for so doing. Thus, if a person was convicted on the basis of an Act which, at the time of trial, they did not seek to challenge, the conviction would stand. The only exception arose where "for wholly exceptional reasons related to some fundamental unfairness" the continued detention would amount to a denial of justice. In this case, the court agreed that no injustice would result from continued incarceration. Hardiman J. noted that even if the defence of mistake had been available, it would not have been open to Mr A. to rely on it, as he was well aware of the age of the victim in this case.

4. ARTICLES 2 AND 3—THE NATION AND THE POSITION OF NORTHERN IRELAND

The Constitution distinguishes between the Nation and the State. A "nation" is a political concept, an idea of a people united by a common identity or by common traits. Such identity may be related to geography, religion, language or race, and may overlap with competing identities, as in Northern Ireland, where two "nations" formerly laid claim to the same territory. A "state" by contrast, is a legal concept, a legal framework by reference to which a territory is governed (see Ch.5 below).

The Irish Nation

Prior to 1999, according to the old Art.2 of the Constitution, the Irish Nation was said to consist of the "whole island of Ireland, its islands and the territorial seas." This controversial provision effectively amounted to a legal claim by the South to the disputed six counties of Northern Ireland. The former Art.3, however, stated that until the national territory was reunited, the laws of the State would apply only to what is generally described as the Republic of Ireland (i.e. the 26 counties). In other words, while the Irish State was considered to have jurisdiction over the whole island, its legal jurisdiction could ordinarily be exercised only in respect of the 26 counties of the Republic of Ireland (see, for instance, *McGimpsey v Ireland* [1990] 1 I.R. 110).

The Good Friday Agreements

The Good Friday Agreements of 1998 changed all this. After decades of violence and political stasis, the various parties in Northern Ireland agreed a compromise that settled how that jurisdiction would be governed. Northern Ireland was granted its own Assembly and a "power-sharing" government consisting of representatives of both traditions in the province. A North-South Ministerial Council was established with representatives from both the North and the South agreeing on strategies of common interest to both jurisdictions.

As part of this settlement, the Government of Ireland promised a referendum on Arts 2 and 3 with a view to removing the legal claim over Northern Ireland. In the ensuing referendum, the People, by an overwhelming margin, passed the Nineteenth Amendment of the Constitution. This amendment proposed the alteration of Arts 2 and 3 of the Constitution with a view to dropping the legal claim over Northern Ireland. This alteration, however, was stated to be conditional upon a government order being made, which occurred on the establishment of a power-sharing Assembly and Government in Northern Ireland and the parallel establishment of the North-South Ministerial Council. When this body finally first met, in early December 1999, the Government passed a resolution bringing the new Arts 2 and 3 into being.

What do the new Articles 2 and 3 say?

Under the new Art.2 of the Constitution (as amended in 1999), the following persons may claim to be part of the Irish nation:

- all persons born on the island of Ireland (or on its islands and seas) have an "entitlement and birthright" to be part of the Irish nation; and
- all persons who, though not born on the island, are qualified to be citizens of Ireland are also entitled to be part of the Irish nation.

Article 2 is very carefully worded. Nationhood is not to be forced on those on our island who claim a different nationality.

The new Art.3 contains similarly conciliatory changes. The key element in this context is that the new Articles drop the legal claim over Northern Ireland as asserted by the old Arts 2 and 3. In their place there is now a statement in Art.3 of the "firm will of the Irish nation ... to unite all the people who share the territory of the island of Ireland ...".

To summarise, Art.3 contains:

- a statement of the desire for unity replacing the legal claim over Northern Ireland;
- an acknowledgement that such a united Ireland may only be brought about through peaceful and democratic means;
- an express recognition that there will be no united Ireland until a majority of the people in each jurisdiction (North and South) give their consent to such unification;
- a statement clarifying that until the jurisdictions are reunited, the laws of the State shall ordinarily apply only to the 26 counties of the Republic of Ireland.

What happens if the Northern Ireland agreements fail?

While the coming into force of the new Articles was conditional upon the setting up of the institutions envisaged by the Good Friday Agreements, their continuation in force is not conditional upon the survival of those institutions. Thus, now that the new Articles are in force, they can only be removed by the People in referendum.

Subsequent progress

The path to power-sharing in fact proved rather rocky. Concerns regarding the alleged activity of paramilitary organisations dogged the Executive for some years. After a period of two years of self-government, the Northern Ireland institutions were suspended in 2002, with power in respect of the jurisdiction being restored to the London Government. In May 2007, however, an agreement by the IRA to cease all activity led to a new power-sharing arrangement and the restoration of devolution. To date, the Northern Ireland institutions appear to be operating as intended.

5. THE IRISH STATE

What is a state?

A state is a legal framework of governance by reference to which a particular geographical territory is run. A state, then, effectively comprises of a system of government, a set of institutions and functionaries that are responsible for regulating the affairs of a defined jurisdiction. A state may or may not be entirely independent. It may, for example, form part of a federation. The state of Wisconsin, for instance, forms part of the federation that is the United States of America. The federal government of the US has several defined powers in respect of each of the constituent states of the US. In a somewhat similar manner, the Irish State is part of the European Union, which is entitled to exercise certain powers in respect of our jurisdiction (See Art.29.4).

The attributes of the Irish State

The name of the State

Article 4 of the Constitution indicates that the name given to the State governing our 26-county jurisdiction is "Ireland" or "Éire". Although the Republic of Ireland Act 1948 designates the State as a "Republic", this does not alter the name of the State, which remains as outlined in Art.4. (At international meetings involving the State, the State is officially designated as "Éire-Ireland".)

The State has separate legal personality

It is useful to compare the State to an incorporated company. The "shareholders" of the company are the People of Ireland, its citizens. The People have created the State by means of the Constitution. In that Constitution, they have outlined definitively how that State is to be run, what roles are to be given to its respective functionaries, and what its overall objects and purpose will be. They have also outlined certain things that the State cannot do. Although the State is run on a day-to-day basis by the Government ("the board of directors"), Art.6 makes it clear that it is the responsibility of the People to decide who will be the rulers of the State, and "in final appeal" to determine "all questions of national policy".

Like a company, however, the State has a legal personality separate from the People who have created or who "own" the State. This means that for legal purposes the State is treated as if it were a separate legal "person". Thus:

*   the State can be sued as a separate person (see *Byrne v Ireland* [1972] I.R. 241);
*   the State can sue other persons as a separate person (see *Ireland v Mulvey, Irish Times*, November 11, 1989));
*   the State can enter into contracts for the purchase of items;
*   the State can own property in its own right (see *Comyn v Attorney General* [1950] I.R. 142).

The State is a democracy

Article 5 of the Constitution stipulates that Ireland is a "democratic State". The State is run in accordance with the Constitution laid down by the People. Its President and lawmakers are chosen by election of the People. Democratically elected members of the Dáil select its Government. The State, moreover, is run in accordance with the rule of law. This means that the State can only do what it is entitled to do under publicly promulgated laws made in accordance with the Constitution.

Is the State a republic?

Effectively, yes. The Republic of Ireland Act 1948 expressly designates the State as a Republic. A "republic", in short, is a state where the People rather than a monarch (king or queen) are said to be sovereign. Although the State is not described in the Constitution as such, the fact that we elect our head of state, the President, on merit, sets us apart from monarchies, where heads of state owe their position solely to the circumstances of their birth. Indeed, in *Howard v Commissioners of Public Works* [1994] 1 I.R. 101, Denham J. remarked that certain royal powers that derived from the position of the monarch in England offended the "republican" principles on which our State is founded. Another key feature of a republic is that the powers of government are typically divided between various named bodies in what is called the "separation of powers" (see below at Ch.7). That said, the official name of the State does not contain the word "Republic". This use of the latter term in the 1948 Act is said to be a *description* of the State rather than an alteration of its title.

Is the State "independent"?

Although Art.5 declares that the State is "independent", this is qualified considerably by Ireland's membership of the European Union. Article 29 of the Constitution permits the State to be a full member of this Union. This means that the laws of the European Union and judgments of the European Courts of Justice and First Instance have legal effect within this State, regardless of the will of the Oireachtas. (See Ch.6 below).

The royal prerogatives and the "sovereignty" of the State

Is the State sovereign?

First, one must define the word "sovereign":

> **Definition:** To be sovereign in the widest sense entails being entirely free from outside control or interference. A "sovereign" can do as he, she or it pleases, without fear of being reprimanded or of having a decision reversed or set aside. In respect of a territory, thus, sovereignty involves having the supreme and unqualified power to rule as one pleases. Sovereignty therefore involves the state of being *answerable to no higher body.*

In the United Kingdom, theoretically, the Crown holds the "sovereign power". This means, technically, that the King or Queen of England has ultimate and supreme power in respect of the UK. Modern realities, of course, dictate that these powers be exercised by elected representatives in Britain. Yet this does not take away from the ultimate sovereignty of the Queen.

Ireland, of course, is a Republic. Here we reject the concept of all power residing in one unelected individual. In Ireland thus it is the People, and not any king or queen, who are "sovereign". The State, being the creation of the People, is not sovereign. The State is after all subject to an external control, the Constitution. The Constitution requires that the State perform certain tasks in a prescribed way. The Constitution, moreover, prevents the State from doing certain things, like creating a death penalty (Art.15.5.2). The State thus is subject to the will of the People as expressed in the Constitution. It cannot hence be described as truly sovereign.

So why does Article 5 describe the State as "sovereign"?

If the State is sovereign, it is sovereign only in a particular and limited manner. The scheme of the Constitution makes it clear that the State is subject to the will of the People. It must obey their Constitution.

The State, for instance, is not immune from being sued in the courts. If it was truly "sovereign", the State could not be sued in this manner. In fact, as part of his sovereign power, the King of England, in 1937 at least, enjoyed what was called a "royal prerogative" right not to be sued. (But see the (British) Crown Proceedings Act 1947, which qualified that right.) A royal prerogative right is a right that the King enjoyed flowing from the fact that he was sovereign. For a long time the State assumed that it was the successor to the King and thus that it also enjoyed such prerogative rights.

Definition: A royal prerogative right is a right that the King or Queen of England enjoys as a consequence of his or her sovereignty. These rights included (before 1947 at least) the right not to be sued, the right to "treasure trove" (to claim items of national heritage), the right to disobey the Crown's own laws, and the right not to have to reveal the content of government documents to a court (the "executive privilege").

In *Byrne v Ireland* [1972] I.R. 241, however, the Supreme Court ruled that the State was not the successor to the Crown and thus did not enjoy these royal prerogatives. The court's reasoning for so ruling was that as the People (and *not* the State) held the "sovereign" power, the State could not claim to have been the successor to the sovereign rights of the King. *Byrne* concerned a claim by the State that it was immune from being sued for negligence by a woman injured when she fell on a public footpath. The court ruled that the State was not immune from suit. The State did not, in particular, enjoy any royal prerogative right as, unlike the King, it was not sovereign. If anyone enjoyed this prerogative it was the People and not the State.

In the same year the Supreme Court ruled that the Government did not enjoy any royal prerogative of "executive privilege" (which had allowed the Government to refuse to produce any State documents in evidence required by a court). In *Murphy v Dublin Corporation* [1972] I.R. 215, the court thus concluded that the executive could not ordinarily prevent the courts using Government documents as evidence in court proceedings.

Another royal prerogative of the King arose for consideration in *Webb v Ireland* [1988] I.R. 353. In that case the plaintiffs had discovered the famous "Derrynaflan Hoard", consisting of a chalice and paten dating back at least 1,300 years. The State claimed that as part of the royal prerogative of "treasure trove", these items of national heritage belonged to the State. The Supreme Court again noted that the State did not enjoy any royal prerogative powers. The State thus was not the successor to any prerogative of treasure trove. (Nevertheless the court found, *on the basis of the Constitution alone,* that these items did belong to the State.)

The State does not, moreover, enjoy any prerogative right to disobey its own laws. In *Howard v Commissioners of Public Works* [1994] 1 I.R. 101, the Supreme Court ruled that (in the absence of an express legal exemption) the State was obliged to seek planning permission for buildings just like anybody else. The court again reiterated the fact that the State is not sovereign.

The concept of "external sovereignty"

The only feasible explanation for Art.5 asserting that the State is sovereign is that the term "sovereign" is used in a limited sense. It is suggested that the term "sovereign" in Art.5 denotes that the State is "externally sovereign". This means that *as against every other State on the globe,* the State called Ireland has the exclusive authority to rule the territory of Ireland. No other State can make laws for our territory. This was confirmed in *Crotty v An Taoiseach* [1987] I.R. 713, where the Supreme Court ruled that only the Government of this State could determine the foreign policy of Ireland. Ordinarily no other State may determine Ireland's foreign policy.

Citizenship

While the laws of Ireland generally apply to all human persons in the State at any particular time, some specific rights and duties apply exclusively to persons who are citizens of Ireland. In particular, only citizens may vote in presidential elections and in referenda. Generally, only citizens are eligible to serve on a jury. A citizen of Ireland owes, under Art.9.3, a duty of fidelity to the nation and loyalty to the State.

Article 9 of the Constitution broadly leaves it to the Oireachtas to determine the conditions under which a person may claim Irish citizenship. Under Art.9 however, the Oireachtas is precluded from denying citizenship on the basis of a person's sex. Women and men alike are equally entitled to claim Irish citizenship. Likewise any person who held citizenship of Saorstát Éireann is also constitutionally entitled to Irish citizenship.

Otherwise, citizenship is determined in accordance with legislation. Under legislation currently in force, a person may acquire citizenship in one of a number of ways, principally:

- By birth on the island of Ireland, subject to the conditions noted below.
- By parentage, i.e. where a child is born outside the island of Ireland, she may nonetheless claim citizenship if one or both of her parents is an Irish citizen.
- By marriage to an Irish citizen or, alternatively, by naturalisation (provided in both cases that certain conditions as to residence and character are met).

Under citizenship legislation, any child born on the island of Ireland prior to January 1, 2005 was entitled automatically to claim citizenship of Ireland. It was widely believed that the amendment of Arts 2 and 3 of the Constitution in 1999 copperfastened this right, giving every person born in Ireland (North or South) an automatic right to claim citizenship. This model of citizenship adhered to the principle of *jus soli*, whereby all persons were entitled as of right to claim citizenship simply by virtue of their birth on the island.

In 2004, however, the Constitution was amended by the Twenty-Seventh Amendment, restricting the automatic right to claim citizenship. The Amendment states that unless otherwise provided for in legislation, a child born in the island of Ireland after the enactment of the Amendment will only be entitled to claim citizenship if, at time of the child's birth, at least one of his parents is a citizen of Ireland.

The Irish Nationality and Citizenship Act 2004, while widening citizenship beyond the scope of the Amendment, nonetheless precludes a child born on or after January 1, 2005, from acquiring citizenship unless, at the time of birth, at least one of his parents is:

- a citizen of Ireland (or a person entitled to Irish citizenship);
- a citizen of the United Kingdom (or a person entitled to British citizenship);
- a person entitled under law to remain indefinitely in either the State or in Northern Ireland;
- a person who has legally resided in the State for at least three of the four years prior to the birth of the child. (For this purpose, time spent as an asylum seeker, a student or an illegal migrant does not count.)

In practice if one of the child's parents is a national of any Member State of the EU or of the European Economic Area (such persons being entitled to work in the State without restriction) the child will be entitled to claim citizenship. Otherwise the child will only become a citizen if either of its parents is legally entitled to remain in the State without restriction as to duration, or has been legally resident here for three of the previous four years. While the child may feasibly acquire citizenship through naturalisation, the automatic right to citizenship on birth has been significantly limited.

6. IRELAND IN THE INTERNATIONAL ORDER

Although Ireland subscribes to the general principles of international law, international agreements do not form part of Irish domestic law. This means that as a general rule, the terms of international agreements cannot be pleaded in a court of law in Ireland unless they have been incorporated into national law by the Oireachtas. In this sense Ireland is said to be a "dualist" rather than a "monist" state.

General principles

Dualism and monism

A dualist state regards international law (including agreements between nations) as an area of law entirely separate from national or domestic law. Ireland is a dualist state. This means that unless an international agreement is made part of national law by the Oireachtas it cannot be pleaded in an Irish court of law (see Art.29.6).

A monist state, on the other hand, does not distinguish between international and national law. International law, in other words, automatically becomes part of national law in a monist state. In particular, a monist state considers both types of law to be enforceable in its national courts, regardless of origin. The Netherlands is a good example of a monist state.

Examples of dualism in Ireland

Article 29.6 stipulates that "… no international agreement shall be part of the domestic law of the State save as may be determined by the Oireachtas". This means that unless an international agreement has been incorporated into Irish law by an Act of the Oireachtas, it cannot be pleaded in an Irish court of law. According to Fennelly J. in *Kavanagh v Governor of Mountjoy Prison* [2002] 3 I.R. 97, Art.29 does not confer on individuals any rights flowing from international law. It concerns the relationship between Ireland and other States as opposed to the relationship between this State and its citizens. As such, unless the Oireachtas decides otherwise, an individual citizen making a claim against the State cannot invoke the principles of international law. (They are not 'justiciable'). International law, in other words, does not in itself create individual rights that can be relied upon by citizens in the Irish courts.

Example: In *Re Ó Láighléis* [1960] I.R. 93, for instance, the plaintiff was prevented from pleading the terms of the European Convention on Human Rights to challenge the reasons for his detention without trial. This case was heard at a time before the Convention was incorporated into Irish law by the European Convention on Human Rights Act 2003. The Supreme Court ruled that because the Convention had not (at that time) been incorporated into Irish law, it could not be taken into account by the court.

Example: Similarly, in *O'B. v S.* [1984] I.R. 316, the Supreme Court refused to consider whether a law that discriminated against children born outside marriage was contrary to the European Convention on Human Rights. Again, the court reasoned that without express incorporation into Irish law, the Convention could not be invoked in an Irish court.

This matter has most recently been considered in *Horgan v Ireland* [2003] 2 I.R. 468. Here an individual citizen claimed that the use of Shannon airport as a 'stopover' for US troops and aircraft engaged in the war in Iraq infringed the principles of international law. Although it permits such stopovers, Ireland is formally neutral in relation to the specific conflict. The Supreme Court accepted that the customary principles of international law prevented the state from allowing troops and munitions to transit through a neutral state on their way to the scene of war. It nonetheless ruled that as this principle had not been incorporated into national law, the plaintiff could not invoke it in support of his claim.

Reliance on judgments of international courts

Even where an international court has handed down a judgment on an issue concerning an Irish citizen, such a judgment is still not part of Irish law unless the specific convention has been incorporated into domestic law.

Example: For instance, in *Norris v Ireland* (1989) 13 E.H.R.R. 186 (decided before the European Convention on Human Rights was incorporated into Irish Law) the plaintiff challenged before the European Court of Human Rights certain Irish laws that banned all forms of male homosexual sexual activity. The European Court ruled that these Irish laws infringed the plaintiff's right to privacy under

Art.8 of the Convention on Human Rights. Nonetheless, these impugned laws remained in force in Ireland until 1993, when the Oireachtas passed the Criminal Law (Sexual Offences) Act 1993. It was only then (when the Oireachtas had acted to incorporate the ruling) that Irish domestic law was altered to comply with the Convention.

That said, in some cases international agreements have been regarded as "persuasive" in interpreting Irish law: see *Ó Domhnaill v Merrick* [1985] I.R. 151 and *Desmond v Glackin (No. 1)* [1993] 3 I.R. 1. In other words, such agreements may be used to cast light on the meaning of Irish legislation, especially considering that the State is bound, under Art.29, to respect the principles of international law.

European Convention on Human Rights

The position in Irish law of the European Convention on Human Rights is a case in point. Ireland signed up to the Convention in 1955, making it part of international law binding on the State. Before 2003, however, the Convention was not part of Irish law, as the Oireachtas had not incorporated the Convention into domestic law. This meant that the Convention could not be relied on, for instance, in Irish courts.

This has changed, however, with the implementation by the Oireachtas of the European Convention on Human Rights Act 2003. This Act requires that to the extent that it is possible to do so, Irish legislation must be interpreted in such a way as to make it consistent with the Convention. Where this is not possible, and the measure is found to infringe the Convention, a declaration of incompatibility can be made. For instance, in *Foy v Registrar of Births, Marriages and Deaths* unreported, High Court, October 19, 2007 and February 15, 2008, McKechnie J. ruled that the refusal of the Registrar to recognize the plaintiff's gender reassignment (the plaintiff, though born anatomically male, identified as female and had surgery giving her the physical attributes of a female) infringed the Convention. On that basis, the judge handed down a declaration of incompatibility. In doing so he followed the Court of Human Rights decision in *Goodwin v United Kingdom* [2002] 35 E.H.R.R. 18 which found that the non-recognition of gender reassignment was in breach of Art.8 of the Convention.

While the incorporation of the Convention has the potential to change Irish law in a significant manner, two points must be noted. First, the incorporation of the Convention is at a 'sub-constitutional' level, in other words it is contained in a piece of legislation that is itself subject to compliance with the Constitution. This means that to the extent that a provision of the Convention conflicts with the Constitution, the Constitution will always prevail. While the Constitution is generally consistent with, and sometimes more protective of rights than the Convention, there are clearly areas, such as the rights of the family, where conflict may arise. Second, the incorporation of the Convention does not in any way undermine the principle that, absent being incorporated into Irish law by the Oireachtas, international law has no standing in Irish courts. To the contrary, it in fact tends to prove the rule given its incorporation by means of the 2003 Act.

Extra-territoriality

As a general rule, Irish law applies only within the confines of the State. There are, however, some cases in which Irish legislation may be applied to situations that arise outside Ireland. While international law generally requires that sovereign states respect each other's boundaries, it recognises the principle of "extra-territoriality", that is, that one state can in limited circumstances apply its laws to incidents that occur in another state.

Example: One good contemporary example of the use of extra-territoriality involves what is sometimes called "sex tourism", where citizens of one state travel to commit a sexual offence in another state, then returning to their state of origin. The Sexual Offences (Jurisdiction) Act 1996 allows Ireland to prosecute persons who have committed a sexual offence while abroad, provided the act is an offence both in Ireland and in the country where it took place. This is possible notwithstanding the fact that, as the offence occurred outside Ireland, the State normally would not have jurisdiction.

Article 29.8 of the Constitution expressly allows Irish legislation to have such "extra-territorial" effects. Given that the State shares a border with Northern Ireland, many of these laws involve relations between the two parts of this island. For instance, the Foyle Fisheries Act 1952 allows fishing offences allegedly committed on the River Foyle (which straddles the border between Derry and Donegal) to be prosecuted in either jurisdiction. In a similar manner (although for different reasons) the Criminal Law Jurisdiction Act 1977 allows certain crimes that have been committed in Northern Ireland to be prosecuted in this State, as if they had occurred here, and vice versa.

It is important to remember, however, that extra-territoriality tends to be the exception rather than the rule. According to the International Court of Justice's decision in the *Lotus Case* (1927) P.C.I.J. Ser. A., No. 10, extra-territorial legislation should only be used where clearly necessary to promote "peace, order and good government" within the state that makes such laws.

The position of the European Union under the Constitution

There is one very significant exception to the principle of dualism. The rule in Art.29.6 (that to become part of Irish law, a provision of international law must be incorporated by the Oireachtas) does not apply to the laws and institutions of what is called the European Union.

What is the European Union?

The European Union is a union of 27 European States committed to economic, social and political co-operation on matters of mutual interest.

In relation to this Union and its rules and principles, two key points need to be made:

- where there is a conflict between the law of the European Union ("EU law") and Irish law, including the Constitution, European Union law always prevails;
- laws made by the European Union may automatically become part of Irish domestic law without the need for incorporation by the Oireachtas.

The supremacy of EU law

In *Campus Oil v Minister for Industry and Energy* (No. 2) [1983] I.R. 88, the Supreme Court ruled that European Union law takes precedence even over the terms of the Constitution. This is in line with EU law itself, which has consistently held that where a conflict exists between national and European Union law, EU law will always prevail (see *Costa v ENEL* [1964] E.C.R. 585). Thus the Supreme Court in *Campus Oil* held that it could not hear an appeal from a decision of the High Court to refer a point of Community law to the European Court of Justice (this being, the Supreme Court thought, contrary to

EU law). Such a result prevailed despite the express terms of Art.34.4.3°, which grants a constitutional right to appeal all decisions of the High Court to the Supreme Court (except where legislation has provided otherwise).

> In cases of conflict between EU law and Irish law, EU law will always prevail. This is the case even where the Irish law concerned is part of the Irish Constitution.

The consensus in the Irish courts on the supremacy of EU law is, however, tempered somewhat by the judgment of Walsh J. in *S.P.U.C. v Grogan* [1989] I.R. 753. In that case, the learned judge suggested that because the amendment affirming the right to life of the unborn child was inserted *after* the amendment allowing Ireland to join the EC, EC law did not prevail over that right to life. Even if this is correct (and, with respect, it more than likely is not an accurate statement of EU law), the subsequent amendments to allow the ratification of amending treaties presumably negate this argument.

Article 29.4.10°: EU measures exempted from compliance with the Constitution

This preference for EU law, even over the terms of the Constitution, is copper-fastened in the Constitution itself by Art.29.4.10°. That provision effectively gives EU law an exemption from having to comply with the Constitution. Thus, an EU provision may become law in Ireland, even where it offends the terms of the Constitution.

Article 29.4.10° basically covers two types of law.

- The first type of law is that created by the institutions of the EU itself. This means that laws made by the EU can become part of Irish law even where they are not in compliance with the Constitution. Article 29.4.10° also allows the measures in question to become part of Irish law notwithstanding the fact that the Oireachtas played no part in their creation. This clearly qualifies Art.15.2, which stipulates that only the Oireachtas may make laws for the State.
- The second type of law exempted under Art.29.4.10° is a law created by the State itself in order to comply with the requirements

of EU law. Where the State enacts a measure that is "necessitated by the obligations of membership" of the EU or the European Communities, that law (and the manner in which it is enacted) need not comply with the requirements of the Constitution.

N.B. If the People approve a proposed referendum allowing the ratification of the Lisbon Treaty, scheduled for June 2008, Art.29.4.10 will be renumbered Art.29.4.9.

Where the State has a discretion in implementing EU law

This exemption, however, only applies to the extent that the State is doing what it is obliged to do by EU law. The State cannot claim such an exemption where it is exercising its own discretion. In other words, if the EU measure does not require the State to take a particular step in implementing an EU measure, the taking of that step does not attract the constitutional exemption envisaged by Art.29.4.10.

Example: In *Greene v Minister for Agriculture* [1990] 2 I.R. 17, the State was obliged by EU law to make certain payments to farmers in disadvantaged areas. The State decided that, for this purpose, persons would be means-tested, in other words farmers would only receive payment if their income was below a certain amount. This means test, however, turned out to be unconstitutional, because it unfairly privileged unmarried farmers over their married counterparts, thereby amounting to an attack on the institution of marriage (see below at pp.166–167). Because the relevant EU Directive did not require the State to discriminate against married farmers, the State could not claim an exemption under (what is now) Art.29.4.10°. The discrimination in question had not been necessitated by EU membership.

The direct effect of EU law

Specific measure of European Union law may become part of Irish law without ever having been approved by the Oireachtas. This is an exception to the general rule, laid out in Art.15.2, that only the Oireachtas may legislate for this State. Thus, by contrast with the provisions of most international agreements, EU law is automatically incorporated into national law. In other words, it has "direct applicability". It can, furthermore, have "direct effects", allowing ordinary individuals to rely on EU law as giving them rights that may be successfully invoked in Irish courts, notwithstanding the fact that the Oireachtas has not approved the creation of such legislation. The net effect is that laws can be created that are applicable in Ireland by a process that effectively "by-passes" the Oireachtas.

The European Communities Act 1972. This "direct effect" is permitted by Art.29.4.10° but is further facilitated by the European Communities Act 1972 (as amended). Section 2 of that Act states that with effect from January 1, 1973, the law of the European Communities "… [s]hall be binding on the State and shall be part of the domestic law thereof under the conditions laid down in [the treaties founding those Communities]".

Section 2, then, automatically makes Community law part of Irish law. This allows an individual to rely on European law in an Irish court to give them legal rights, powers or immunities that they otherwise would not have.

Implementing EU legislation in Ireland

Special constitutional considerations apply where legislation passed by the EU institutions is required to be transposed into Irish law by means of Irish legislation. Where there is a choice of legislative methods (primary or secondary legislation) for transposition, the question arises as to what method is to be preferred. This matter is dealt with below at pp.66–68.

Is a referendum required every time there is a new EU Treaty?

In the course of its history the EU has developed considerably. The original scope of the first treaties has been significantly extended by a series of amending treaties, the most prominent of which are the Single European Act 1986, the Maastricht Treaty 1992, the Amsterdam Treaty 1997 and most recently the Nice Treaty 2001. A referendum on the ratification of the Lisbon Treaty 2007 is scheduled for June 2008.

Once signed by the State, an "amending" treaty does not come into effect until every state that has signed it "ratifies" (i.e. endorses) the treaty in accordance with its own constitutional requirements. In theory, any state (including Ireland) may refuse to ratify a treaty even after it has been signed. In other words, Ireland is never obliged to ratify an amending treaty: it may always choose to do otherwise. As a result it cannot be said that ratifying these treaties is "necessitated by the obligations of membership of the European Union" (and thus exempted from having to comply with the Constitution).

Do we thus need a new referendum for every change in the treaties of the European Communities and Union? In *Crotty v An Taoiseach* [1987] I.R. 713, Finlay C.J. noted that the European Communities are dynamic in nature and must be expected to change and develop over time. When the Irish people passed the Third Amendment, allowing the State to join the Communities, such change must have been anticipated. To the extent, therefore, that the proposed reforms to those Communities remained within the broad "purpose and objectives" of the original treaties, the Chief Justice agreed that the changes introduced by the amending treaty would be protected by the Constitution. If however, the changes in question altered the essential scope of the original objectives and aims of the Communities, they would not be afforded an exemption from the terms of the Constitution. In other words, a referendum may be required where seriously ground-breaking changes are being proposed. Otherwise such changes would not attract the constitutional exemption afforded by Art.29.4.

Applied to the various treaties passed since 1987, it might be said that the Maastricht Treaty, having made very significant alterations to the Communities, did require a referendum to give it constitutional immunity. The impact of the Amsterdam and Nice Treaties, however, is generally acknowledged as being less dramatic and as such, these Treaties *may* not have required referenda. That said, both treaties were subjected to a popular vote in referendum—the State has tended to "play it safe" when it comes to the constitutional validity of changes to the EU structures.

In short, if the proposed amendment to the EU is merely a development within the original aims and objectives of the Communities and Union, no referendum will be required. If, however, the proposed changes significantly alter the purpose or powers of the Communities and Union, a new referendum will be required.

7. THE SEPARATION OF POWERS

A fundamental aspect of Irish constitutional law is the doctrine of the separation of powers. It may be appropriate to introduce the issue at this point. It is also dealt with in more detail below in the chapters on the Oireachtas, the Government and the courts respectively. While those chapters deal with the different elements in more detail, a general understanding of the operation of the separation of powers is essential to an appreciation of the functioning of the various institutions and their relationship with each other.

The principle of the separation of powers requires that the various powers of the State be divided on a pre-arranged basis between the different organs of State. Each organ of State is thus said to have exclusive powers that only it can exercise. Any attempt by one institution of State (or for that matter by a body that is not an institution of State) to invoke or use powers exclusively reserved to another institution would constitute an unconstitutional "invasion" of the powers of that body. The reason for such separation lies in the perceived danger of residing all State power in one person or body alone, with the attendant likelihood of corruption and abuse of power by that person or body. Thus the institutions of State are said to exercise their powers in a manner that provides a system of checks and balances, each institution supervising and overseeing the activities of the others.

Typically the powers of the State are divided between:

1. a "legislature", which performs the law-making power (in Ireland this power is exercised by Parliament, or, as it is better known, the Oireachtas);
2. an "executive", or Government that administers and oversees on a day-to-day basis the operation and implementation of laws made the legislature; and
3. a "judiciary", that is, judges administering justice in courts of law; this comprises, in particular, adjudicating in disputes as to the meaning and application of the law.

The legislative role—making law

The national Parliament (the Oireachtas) has certain exclusive powers that only it may exercise. Indeed, Art.15.2 of the Constitution states

49

that only the Oireachtas can make laws in respect of the State. No other legislative body (except those of the European Union) may create laws applicable within the State. In particular, restrictions apply in relation to the delegation of legislative powers by the Oireachtas to other bodies, such as the Government. Under the Constitution itself, furthermore, Parliament and its members enjoy certain privileges that, for instance, prevent the courts from intervening in the internal workings of the Houses of the Oireachtas. Members are privileged (i.e. not answerable to a court), moreover, in respect of their utterances before either House.

Courts do not make law

Much of the case law on this point addresses the reluctance of the courts to make policy or law for the State. The Supreme Court noted in *Norris v Attorney General* [1984] I.R. 36 that it does not engage in law reform. In other words, the courts consider that in performing their functions, they are limited to stating what the law is, rather than what it ought to be. Thus in *McGrath v McDermott* [1988] I.L.R.M. 647, the Supreme Court refused to accept that it could "add to or delete from" legislative provisions with a view to closing off loopholes in the tax code. To do so, it said, would involve altering the law of the State, a function that is reserved solely to the Oireachtas.

State (Murphy) v Johnston [1983] I.R. 235 clearly establishes that a court cannot change legislation so as to rectify even an obvious error in such measures. In this case, the High Court refused to amend legislation so as to alter a mistake in cross-referencing between sections, ruling that only the Oireachtas had the power to alter legislation in this manner.

This reluctance on the part of the courts to fix legislation is mirrored in *C.C. v Ireland (No. 2)* [2006] I.E.S.C. 33. There the Supreme Court struck down a law banning sexual intercourse with a girl under the age of 15, on the ground that the law did not afford a defence of mistake as to the age of the girl. Having so ruled, the court declined to issue an order in terms that would have upheld the relevant section subject to the inclusion of such a defence. This, Hardiman J., ruled, would have involved the court in "a process akin to legislation", which was the job not of the courts but of the legislature. Given also, that there were a variety of ways in which such a defence might be framed, the court felt it was inappropriate for them to choose how the defence would be introduced.

Behind this reluctance lies a democratic imperative. The People of Ireland elect TDs (and indirectly elect Senators) to make laws and policy for the State. If they do not approve of the policy made by those legislators, the People are free to remove the latter at subsequent elections. By contrast, judges are not elected and remain, moreover, independent in the performance of their roles. They, quite rightly, cannot be removed for making a decision of which the People disapprove. Many commentators thus argue that judges should leave policy-making to the elected Parliament.

The executive role—governing the State, administering the operation of laws

The Government too enjoys certain powers that are not extended to other functionaries. For instance, the sole and exclusive power to determine the State's foreign policy is reserved to the Government (see *Crotty v An Taoiseach* [1987] I.R. 713). Similarly in *Horgan v Ireland* [2003] 2 I.R. 468 and *Dubsky v Ireland* [2005] I.E.H.C. 442 the courts stressed their reluctance to intervene in the thorny matter of the State's apparent facilitation of the US military in allowing stopovers at Shannon airport en route to the conflicts in Iraq and Afghanistan respectively. Such matters, the court believed, fell within the exclusive function of the Executive in relation to the conduct of foreign affairs. The courts would only interfere, they said, where there was a clear and serious disregard of the Constitution.

Arguably, the principle of cabinet confidentiality reflects also the reluctance of judges to interfere in the functioning of the Government, by protecting the right of the Government to preserve the secrecy of its deliberations (Art.28.4.3). (See below at pp.66–68).

The judicial role—interpreting and enforcing law

By the same token, the judicial role (as we will see in Ch.13) is deemed to be the sole preserve of the courts. Article 34.1 ascribes the sole and exclusive power to "administer justice" to the judiciary (judges) in courts of law. Thus, subject to the provisions of Art.37, no one other than a judge may determine the results of legal disputes or impose legal liabilities or penalties on litigants or accused persons. Article 35.2 moreover asserts that in the performance of their role judges are independent of all save the "Constitution and the law". Thus, for instance, in *Buckley v Attorney General* [1950] I.R. 67, an

Act of the Oireachtas purporting to suspend a case before the High Court and to impose a legislative result in that case was struck down as unconstitutional. Once a case is pending before a court, the Supreme Court held, it can only be decided by a judge, and not by Act of Parliament.

The courts have also been quite assertive in confirming that the imposition of a sentence on conviction of a particular offender is a matter exclusively for the courts. (See below at pp.101–103).

Checks and balances: some cracks in the separation of powers doctrine

The separation of powers in Ireland, however, is not applied quite as rigidly as might first appear. The relationship between the various arms of the State is in fact quite complex, involving a delicate series of checks and balances. Not least among these is the power of judicial review explicitly afforded to the courts by the Constitution (See Ch.3 below). The courts have a right, after all, to review the constitutionality of measures taken by both the Oireachtas and Executive, striking down unconstitutional provisions. Similarly:

•   The Government of the State is not in fact fully independent of the other institutions of State. The Government after all is effectively "hired and fired" by the Dáil (see Arts 13.1.1°–2° and Arts 28.10–11).

•   The Government, moreover, is answerable to the Dáil for its decisions (Art.28.4). Thus the Government depends on the Dáil not only for its initial creation but also for its continued survival. In addition, the Taoiseach (being the Head of Government) requires, for his appointment, the support of a majority of Dáil members. He can, furthermore, be forced to resign if he loses that support during his time in office (see below at pp.84–86).

•   The Taoiseach, in turn, has some role in the selection of Members of Parliament. The Taoiseach first elected after a general election appoints eleven members of the Seanad. This usually secures for the Government of the day a majority in that House (see below pp.78–79).

•   Although judges are independent in the performance of their functions (Art.35.2), the President appoints all judges, effectively on the instructions of the Government (see Art.35.1 and Art.13.9). (In practice, most judicial appointments are made on

the advice of an independent Judicial Appointments Advisory
Board.)

• The Oireachtas is also empowered to impeach (remove from office)
a judge or the President for stated incapacity or misbehaviour.

• The courts themselves in turn supervise the activities of the
Government and the Oireachtas, by means of judicial review (see
above in Ch.3).

Socio-economic rights and the distribution of resources

In certain contexts, however, the separation of powers is observed
particularly strictly. Judges are especially reluctant to rule on matters
that affect the way in which the State's financial and other resources
are distributed. They are, moreover, largely unwilling to enforce what
are claimed to be socio-economic rights, such as the right to adequate
housing, food or sustenance. The court will only intervene, according
to the Supreme Court in *T.D. v Minister for Education* [2001] 4 I.R.
259, where the conduct of either the Oireachtas or Government results
in a "conscious and deliberate breach" of a constitutional right.

The courts generally take the view that the distribution of the
State's financial resources lies within the exclusive remit of the elected
legislature and not that of the courts. The power to determine how
state revenue will be collected, and how it will be spent is reserved to
the Oireachtas, and more specifically the Dáil. While it is possible for
the courts to restore parties' legal entitlements (the process of
'commutative justice') decisions involving the redistribution of
existing wealth patterns (achieving 'distributive justice') are left to the
Dáil. This is sometimes termed the 'deferential' approach, noting the
deference that the courts accord to the Oireachtas in the performance
of its legislative functions.

For instance, in *O'Reilly v Limerick Corporation* [1989] I.L.R.M.
181, Costello J. refused to order the State to provide basic amenities
(such as running water to members of the Travelling Community). To
do so, the judge reasoned, would involve the court ordering the State
to spend finite resources in a particular way, a matter peculiarly within
the province of elected representatives. While the courts concern
themselves with specific instances of alleged injustice, the Oireachtas
has to consider the overall distribution of wealth, in situations where
there are many competing demands for limited state resources. (In
other words, if a court were to rule that money be spent in a particular

way, how would it decide from where that money would come? Who would in turn be deprived of those resources?)

T.D. v Minister for Education [2001] 4 I.R. 259 involved one of a number of troubled youths, who required specialised secure care facilities. At that time, the State had no such facility. In the High Court, Kelly J. had ordered the State to establish a secure unit to contain and support these young persons. The Supreme Court, however, reversed this order, noting that the establishment and funding of such units was a matter for the legislature and the executive, and not for the courts. Allocating State funds, the Supreme Court reasoned, was not a matter that the courts were either entitled or equipped to do. The Supreme Court thus ruled that Kelly J. had infringed the separation of powers doctrine, as the courts could not dictate how the wealth of the State be distributed. (See also the similar reasoning applied in *Sinnott v Minister for Education* [2001] 2 I.R. 545)

Likewise, in *Re Article 26 and the Health (Amendment) (No. 2) Bill 2004* [2005] I.E.S.C. 7, the Supreme Court concluded that there was no constitutional right to free residential medical care for elderly and infirm persons. Thus it was not unconstitutional generally to impose charges in respect of residential care facilities, provided the charges only applied from the date on which the Bill came into force. The court noted that there were, in the Bill, sufficient measures to prevent hardship arising to especially vulnerable or deprived people. (Nonetheless, retrospective measures seeking to excuse illegal charges collected in the past were deemed unconstitutional, being an infringement of the property right to sue for moneys paid in breach of the law).

Nevertheless, in both *T.D.* and the *Health Amendment* reference, the Supreme Court noted that there were limits to the reticence of the courts. While the courts generally lean against asserting socio-economic rights, and intervening in relation to the appropriate allocation of resources, Judges reserve their right to step in where there is a "conscious and deliberate breach" of a constitutional right. This admittedly requires something in the nature of bad faith or recklessness, but it nonetheless underlines that the courts could, in appropriately extreme cases, uphold a socio-economic right, even if this involved trampling on the Oireachtas' sole right to determine the proper distribution of state resources.

8. THE PRESIDENT

Introduction

What is the President?

Although not described as such in the Constitution, the President is the head of state in Ireland. A "head of state" is ordinarily a figurehead who occupies a formal role as leader of a state but who typically has little or no power in its running. Some other European states (e.g. the UK, The Netherlands, Norway) have a monarch (king or queen) as head of state, a person who attains such title by virtue of birth and heredity. The People of Ireland, by contrast, elect their head of state on the basis of merit. This is the hallmark of republican democracy: leaders are chosen by democratic means and on merit, rather than by accident of birth.

While the President is deemed by Art.12 to "take precedence over all other persons in the State", the role of the President is effectively quite limited. The functions of the President can best be described as ceremonial. In particular, the President is expected to be "above politics", and is not ordinarily permitted to take sides in political disputes. This gives the role of President a "unifying" character: the President must be seen to be above the political fray.

How long does a President serve?

Since 1938, there have been eight Presidents, the latest being Her Excellency, Mrs Mary McAleese. The normal term of office of a President lasts seven years. A sitting or former President may be re-elected to that office, but only once. In other words, no person may serve as President for longer than 14 years. Three Presidents (Seán T. Ó Ceallaigh, Éamon de Valera and Patrick Hillery) have served for 14 years. Additionally, the incumbent President, Mary McAleese, is currently serving her second term, having been reappointed unopposed in 2004. Of the remaining five, one (Erskine Childers) died one year into his term of office, while another (Cearbhall Ó Dálaigh) resigned after two years as President. The President may lose office if he or she dies, resigns or is removed from office by the Oireachtas, for stated misbehaviour. (See Art.12.3 and the discussion at p.59). The President may also be removed if permanently incapacitated, such incapacity being confirmed by a Supreme Court consisting of not less than five judges. (See Art.12.3).

Electing the President

Eligibility

Any citizen of Ireland aged 35 or over is eligible to be elected President (Art.12.4). In order to run for election, however, a person must be nominated in the manner set out in Art.12.4. This provides three options for nomination:

* a person may be nominated by not less than 20 sitting members of the Oireachtas (i.e. of the Dáil and/or Seanad);
* alternatively, a person may be nominated by not less than four county or borough councils (e.g. Clare County Council, Waterford City Council);
* an outgoing (retiring) President may nominate himself or herself (subject to the requirement that a President may serve no more than two terms in office).

There is no restriction on a person born outside the State serving as President, provided he or she is a citizen at the time of election. President Éamon de Valera, for instance, was born in New York, while President McAleese hails from Northern Ireland. President Childers, moreover, was born in London.

Election

If only one candidate's name is put forward, no election is required. Otherwise, the election of a President proceeds by direct vote of the citizens of Ireland. The method of election is the single transferable vote system of proportional representation.

The powers of the President

The powers of the President are significantly limited by the Constitution. Basically, the President cannot ordinarily act otherwise than under instruction from the Government (Art.13.9), although there are several exceptions to this rule. Certain of the President's powers are to be exercised under instruction from the Taoiseach and others under direction from the Dáil. In at least seven specified cases, however, the

President may act at her own discretion, in other words, free of any obligation to obey another person or organ of State.

Cases where the President acts on the instructions of the Dáil

- The President appoints each new Taoiseach on the nomination of the Dáil. Effectively, the President must comply with the choice of Dáil Éireann (Art.13.1.1°).

Cases where the President acts on the instructions of the Taoiseach

- The President summons and dissolves Dáil Éireann on the instructions of the Taoiseach. The President may, however, refuse to follow the Taoiseach's advice where that Taoiseach has lost the support of a majority in the Dáil (Art.13.2.1–2°).
- The President appoints the members of the Government on the instructions of the Taoiseach, though subject to the approval of Dáil Éireann (Art.13.1.2°).
- The President appoints the Attorney General on the instructions of the Taoiseach (Art.30.2).
- The President must terminate the office of a Minister or of the Attorney General if requested to do so by the Taoiseach (Art.28.9.4° and Art.30.5).

Cases where the President acts on the instructions of the Government

- The President is Supreme Commander of the Defence Forces. All commissioned officers of the armed forces are appointed in her name (Art.13.4).
- The President appoints all judges, on the instructions of the Government (Art.35.1).
- Where the President is given any powers under legislation, these powers may only be exercised on the instructions of the Government (Art.13.11).

Cases where the President may act alone

In the following cases, the President may act alone, i.e. entirely at her own discretion. In all but the first and last of these cases, the President must first seek the advice of the Council of State, although in every such case she is free to ignore the advice that it gives her. (Arts 31–32).

- The President may *at her absolute discretion* refuse a Taoiseach's request to dissolve the Dáil, where that Taoiseach has lost the support of a majority of Dáil members (Art.13.2.2°). (The Council of State need not be consulted in relation to this matter). The Constitution does not define what is meant by a loss of majority support in this context, though one might speculate that it would probably be indicated by the loss by the Taoiseach of a vote of confidence, or a defeat of the Government in a vote on a Government-proposed Bill. (This power has yet to be exercised by the President).

- The President may refer a Bill (or part thereof) passed by the Dáil and Seanad to the Supreme Court in order to test its constitutionality (Art.26—see above at pp.17–21).

- The President may establish a Committee of Privileges to determine whether a Bill is a "Money Bill" for the purposes of Arts 21–22 (see below at p.80).

- The President may, in times of emergency, agree to the shortening of the time available for the consideration of a Bill by Seanad Éireann (Art.24).

- The President may address the Houses of the Oireachtas, or the Nation, on a matter of national or public importance. (The content of the address, however, must be pre-approved by the Government.) (Art.13.7). The President is also generally entitled to convene a meeting of either or both Houses of the Oireachtas (Art.13.2).

- Under Art.27, the President may accept a request that an ordinary Bill passed under the provisions of Art.23 of the Constitution be referred to the people in a referendum. A Bill passed under Art.23 is a Bill which has been rejected in the Seanad. After a 90-day delay the Dáil may invoke Art.23, allowing the Bill to be passed by both Houses, notwithstanding the opposition of the Seanad. In response, a majority of the Seanad and at least one-third of the members of the Dáil can jointly petition the President to refer the matter to the People in referendum. If she decides that the Bill raises a matter of sufficient national importance, the President, having consulted with the Council of State, has a discretion to refer the matter to a referendum of the People. Rather unusually, a Bill which is the subject of an Art.27 referendum will be deemed to have passed *unless* the people by a majority representing at least one-third of those entitled to vote *veto* (vote against) the Bill. In other words, unless the required

number of votes is cast against the bill, it will be regarded as
having passed. E.g. if 50 per cent of the electorate votes, and 51
per cent of those voting vote against, the Bill would nonetheless
pass as the number of no votes is less than one-third of the entire
electorate. (To date, Art.27 has never been used.)
* The President may, at her own discretion, appoint up to seven
members of the Council of State. (Art.31.3) (The other members of
the Council need not be consulted in relation to such appointments).

Accountability and impeachment

In respect of the performance of her powers and functions, the President
is not answerable to the Oireachtas or to the courts (Art.13.8). In
O'Malley v An Taoiseach [1990] I.L.R.M. 461, Hamilton P., while
agreeing that the distribution of TDs between electoral constituency
boundaries breached the terms of the Constitution, declined to prevent
the President from dissolving the Dáil on the advice of the Taoiseach,
on the basis that the courts could not interfere in the President's
functions.

The President may, however, be impeached and removed from
office for stated misbehaviour. For this purpose, one House of the
Oireachtas (acting on the basis of at least a two-thirds majority) must
lay a charge before the other House, which that latter House will then
investigate. The President may only be removed by a vote of two-
thirds or more of the members of the latter House. (See Art.12.10).

Those who assist the President

The Council of State

The Council of State is a body that advises the President on matters
relating to the performance of her discretionary powers. In certain
cases, the President is obliged to seek the Council's advice before
acting. In every such case, however, the President is entitled to accept
or reject this advice as she sees fit. In other words, while obliged to
seek the advice of the Council, she is not required to follow such
advice.

The Council of State consists of the following persons:

* The current Taoiseach, Tánaiste, Chief Justice of the Supreme
Court, President of the High Court, Attorney General, and Chair-

persons (the Ceann Comhairle and Cathaoirleach respectively) of Dáil and Seanad Éireann.

* Every past President, Taoiseach, Chief Justice and Prime Minister of the Irish Free State ("President of the Executive Council") still willing and able to sit on the Council.
* Up to seven persons nominated by the President at her own sole discretion.

While the President is generally required to consult with the Council on most matters that are within her discretion, she is not obliged to consult with the Council regarding two matters:

* A decision not to dissolve the Dáil where the Taoiseach has lost the support of a majority in that House;
* The nomination by the President of seven members of the Council of State.

Article 14

In a case where the President is either unable or unwilling to perform her functions, such functions and powers as she enjoys may be exercised by a Commission established under Art.14 of the Constitution. This Commission consists of the Chief Justice of the Supreme Court and the Chairpersons of the Dáil and Seanad respectively. The Commission may act, for instance, where the President is deceased, permanently or temporarily incapacitated, absent from the State, or otherwise simply unable or unwilling to perform her functions.

Summary

The powers of the President are in practice particularly limited. Outside very exceptional circumstances, she usually acts on the "advice" (effectively the instructions) of other organs of State, typically the Government but also the Dáil and the Taoiseach. Articles 13.9 and 13.11 in most cases prevent the President from acting otherwise than under the instructions of the Government. Indeed, even if the President were to refuse to perform a particular task, a Commission established under Art.14 could effectively perform this task in her place.

Nonetheless, in certain cases the President, having taken the advice of the Council of State, may act entirely at her own discretion, although the situations in which this is permitted are very limited. The most important of these is Art.26, which allows the President to refer a Bill to the Supreme Court to determine whether it or any part thereof is repugnant to the Constitution. It is also important to mention the President's power to refuse to dissolve the Dáil where the Taoiseach no longer has majority support in that House. In exercising this specific power, the President need not consult with the Council of State.

The key point, however, is that these powers are the exception rather than the rule.

9. THE OIREACHTAS

The Oireachtas is the National Parliament, the body charged with creating laws for the State. It consists of the President and two Houses, Dáil Éireann (the Lower House, described in the Constitution as the "House of Representatives") and Seanad Éireann (the Upper House, also called the "Senate"). Generally the role of the President is confined to signing and promulgating (putting forward as law) legislation passed by the two Houses. The respective powers of each House are considered below in Ch.10.

The exclusive powers of the Oireachtas: only the Oireachtas may make laws

Article 15.2 states that only the Oireachtas may create laws:

> "The sole and exclusive power of making laws for the State is hereby vested in the Oireachtas; no other legislative authority has power to make laws for the State."

Article 29.6, furthermore, prevents an international agreement from changing Ireland's domestic laws without the consent of the Oireachtas. In other words, an international convention will only become part of Irish law where an Act of Parliament has been enacted incorporating that agreement into national law (see above at pp.40–43).

There is one important exception to this. Article 29.4.10° allows the European Union to make laws that apply in this State, notwithstanding the provisions of Art.15.2. This means that a provision may become part of the law of Ireland even though it has not been approved by the Oireachtas (see above at pp.44–47).

Otherwise, the rule that only the Oireachtas may make laws has important ramifications. It means that neither the Government nor the courts can "usurp" (take over) this role by making laws themselves.

Example: In *Maher v Attorney General* [1973] I.R. 140, the Supreme Court considered the constitutionality of a measure stipulating that the results of a blood sample taken from a person alleged to be driving having taken more than the permitted level of alcohol would be "conclusive evidence" of the driver's guilt. This meant that such evidence could not be challenged in a court of law.

The Supreme Court considered that this was unconstitutional, as it both infringed the alleged offender's right to defend himself and obstructed the courts' role in determining the facts of a case as well as the guilt or innocence of specific defendants in criminal cases.

The court furthermore rejected the suggestion that it should read the legislation as if the term "conclusive" was absent therefrom. While this might have cured the legislation of its unconstitutionality, it would have amounted to an invasion of the Oireachtas's role in making (and changing) legislation. While the courts can interpret (determine the meaning) of legislation, they are not entitled to *change* its meaning outright.

Example: *State (Murphy) v Johnston* [1983] I.R. 235, clearly establishes that a court cannot change legislation so as to rectify even an obvious error in such measures. In this case, the High Court refused to amend legislation so as to alter a mistake in cross-referencing between sections, ruling that only the Oireachtas had the power to alter legislation in this manner.

Example: In *McGrath v McDermott* [1988] I.L.R.M. 647, the Supreme Court refused to accept that it could "add to or delete from" legislative provisions with a view to closing off loopholes in the tax code. To do so, it said, would involve altering the law of the State, a function that is reserved solely to the Oireachtas.

It is worth noting also that the Oireachtas has the exclusive right to raise an army; Art.15.6 bans the establishment and operation of any army not permitted by the Oireachtas.

The Government's role in making law: delegated legislation

Every year the Government ("Executive") passes hundreds of "statutory instruments", ministerial orders that supplement rules laid down in parliamentary legislation. Such instruments are generally technical in nature, containing considerable detail on matters that the Oireachtas might not have the time to consider. The question that arises in this context is whether the making of such instruments constitutes "lawmaking". If the answer to this is yes, then the Government would be engaging in something that only the Oireachtas can do.

It has been held in the courts that the Government can continue to make statutory instruments provided that two conditions are met.

- The statutory instrument must follow the law rather than make new law. This is called the "principles and policies" test.

- The statutory instrument must not attempt to "change, amend or repeal" the law as set out in an Act of Parliament.

The "principles and policies" test

In *Cityview Press v An Comhairle Oiliúna (AnCO)* [1980] I.R. 381, the question arose whether Parliament could delegate certain powers to the defendant body, AnCO, which was at that time responsible for training people for work in various industries. The legislation in question, the Industrial Training Act 1967, had allowed AnCO to set and impose certain levies on industry to help pay for this training. The plaintiff complained that only the legislature (Parliament) could set and impose such levies.

In the Supreme Court, O'Higgins C.J. outlined the following test:

> A power may be delegated by the legislature where it involves *no more than the mere "giving effect" to principles and policies already contained in legislation*. In other words, the Government and other agencies are empowered only to *"fill in the fine details of legislation"* based on and following clearly prescribed pre-existing legislative policies, not to make new legislation or policy for the State.

Example: In *Cityview Press* itself, the Supreme Court ruled that the powers conferred on AnCO by the Act were in keeping with the Constitution. Applying the principles and policies test, the Supreme Court concluded that, in setting and collecting these levies, AnCO was merely following the policy of Parliament and not setting policy on its own. The policy of the State was that employers should pay for the training of workers. AnCO was merely giving effect to this policy.

Example: In *Re Article 26 and the Health (Amendment) (No. 2) Bill 2004* [2005] I.E.S.C. 7, the Supreme Court (while striking down the Bill for other reasons) upheld the delegation of power to the Minister for Health to make regulations for the future imposition of charges for nursing home care. The Bill allowed the Minister, subject to certain exceptions, to set charges for such care, effectively affording her a discretion as to the level of fees to be set. The Supreme Court concluded that this constituted "no more than the implementation of the principles and policies contained in the Act" and was thus permissible. A power given to the CEO of a Health Board to waive or reduce charges in cases of hardship was also upheld.

Example: On the other side of this line stands *Laurentiu v Minister for Justice, Equality and Law Reform* [1999] 4 I.R. 26. In this case the Supreme Court ruled that in determining the criteria upon which non-EU nationals could be deported from the State, the Minister for Justice was in fact making policy, rather than merely giving effect to principles and policies contained in the Aliens Act 1935. The legislature, in passing the Act, conferred on the Minister a general power to make provision for the exclusion and deportation of foreign nationals. In this case there were simply no principles or policies in the legislation for the Minister to follow. The Minister was effectively given the bare power to create these policies himself. This, the court concluded, was unconstitutional.

Example: In *McDaid v Sheehy* [1991] 1 I.R. 1, the High Court ruled that legislation permitting the Government to create and set customs duties involved an unconstitutional delegation of the power to make law. The legislation in question had granted a "bare" power to the Government to impose taxes without reference to any "principles or policies" which such provisions might follow.

It is hard to escape the overall impression that the Oireachtas enjoys a relatively wide latitude in delegating its powers. Provided it has set out some overarching policies or principles that the delegate has to follow, the delegation will be upheld. The result, in practice, is that the centrality of the Oireachtas in the creation of policy has arguably been eroded in favour of the Government. It is clear, nonetheless, that where an Act contains minimal or no principles or policies, leaving a Minister to his or her own devices, the measure will more than likely be unconstitutional.

Changing, amending or repealing legislation

In making statutory instruments, the Government is generally prohibited from changing, amending or repealing (reversing outright) any law set down by the Oireachtas.

Example: In *Cooke v Walsh* [1984] I.R. 710, the Supreme Court ruled that a Minister could not, in a statutory instrument, purport to take away a right that a citizen enjoyed under legislation. In that case, the Minister for Health attempted to deprive the plaintiff of free medical care to which he was entitled under the Health Act 1970. The Supreme Court held that by so acting the Minister had attempted to alter a legislative provision, something that he was not entitled to do.

Example: In *Harvey v Minister for Social Welfare* [1990] 2 I.R. 232, the Supreme Court ruled that the Minister for Social Welfare could not by statutory instrument reverse the plaintiff's entitlement to certain social welfare payments. As that right was guaranteed by a law created by the Oireachtas, the Minister could not alter the plaintiff's right to such payments.

Delegated legislation and the implementation of EU law

As discussed above in Ch.6, measures adopted by the institutions of the European Union generally have direct effect, that is, they apply in Irish law even in the absence of approval from the Oireachtas. Such measures, moreover, take precedence over any conflicting provision of Irish law, including the Constitution itself.

In some cases, however, legislation passed by European Union (EU) institutions requires individual EU Member States to take steps to implement the measures into (make them part of) domestic law. EC Directives are one example of such a law. A Directive is a measure that requires the states to which it is addressed to achieve a particular result as laid out in the text of the Directive. The Member States, however, retain a choice as to how that purpose is to be achieved. Thus Directives, unlike other types of EU law, are not directly applicable. In order to become a full part of national law, they must be implemented into national law by whatever means the Member State chooses (see Art.249, EC Treaty).

By contrast EC Regulations generally apply without the need for incorporation. Nevertheless, in certain cases, EC Regulations may by their terms require the State to take specified steps through the enactment of national legislation.

The net question that arises in this context is whether and to what extent implementation of these EU laws can be achieved by means of delegated legislation. As the State has a choice as to how the implementation occurs, can it be said that the implementation by means of a statutory instrument is justified? Or must the measure be passed by means of an Act of Parliament?

Ireland has chosen to allow the State to implement Directives by means of ministerial order or statutory instrument. Section 3 of the European Communities Act 1972 allows a Minister to implement an EU measure by means of statutory instruments. In doing so the Minister is permitted to vary, alter or repeal any inconsistent piece of legislation, as he or she sees fit (see s.3(2)). This means that measures of EU law may be transposed into national law without having been approved by Parliament. In particular, s.3 allows legislation passed by Parliament to be amended by a Minister of Government. Likewise, the European Communities Act 2007 allows powers to create statutory instruments contained in Acts of Parliament other than the 1972 Act to be used to give effect to EU law in a manner similar to s.3 of the 1972 Act. This can be done where the Act in question deals with substantially the same topic covered in the relevant EU measure. Does this approach offend the doctrine of the separation of powers?

In ordinary circumstances, only the Oireachtas may make law for the State. Therefore any attempt by a Minister to vary laws made by Parliament would normally be regarded as unconstitutional (see above at pp.65–66). In the context of EU law, however, a somewhat more nuanced response is required.

The Irish courts had to consider this issue in *Meagher v Minister for Agriculture* [1994] 1 I.R. 329. In that case, the Minister, in implementing an EC Directive under s.3(2) of the Act of 1972, purported to change part of the Petty Sessions Act 1851. The plaintiff argued that this was unconstitutional, as only the Oireachtas could change legislation. The High Court agreed that unless the exemption in Art.29.4.10° applied, the Minister's action would have been unconstitutional. As Member States had a choice regarding *how* they implemented Directives, it could not be said that Ireland was required to implement Directives by statutory instrument, or indeed by any other specified means. Thus the Minister's unconstitutional actions were not exempted under Art.29.4.10°.

The Supreme Court, however, decided otherwise. While Ireland may not have been strictly obliged to adopt this particular method of implementing Directives, the *practical* reality was that statutory instruments provided the only feasible way of so doing. There are so many Directives that have to be implemented every year, the judges reasoned, that the prospect of implementing them all by Act of Parliament would be unthinkable. The Oireachtas would not feasibly be able to keep up with the pace of change in EU law and Ireland would quickly default in its obligation to implement Directives.

Thus the Supreme Court recognised that the term "necessitated" in Art.29.4.10° had to be read as allowing methods of implementation that were *practically* necessitated in circumstances where a large volume of EU legislation needed to be transposed. As a result, "possibly in a great majority of" (though notably not *all*) cases the implementation of EU Law could be achieved by means of a statutory instrument. The court further considered that the Minister was justified in concluding that the amendment of the Petty Sessions Act was justified in order to give effect to the enforcement of EU law.

To this, however, an important caveat must be added. Where the EC Directive (or EC Regulation) itself leaves to the Member States a discretion to create certain principles and policies, an Act of Parliament *will* be required for the State to exercise such a discretion. In most cases, Directives and certainly EC Regulations are clear as to the principles and policies involved. As such, the State usually is involved only in giving effect to these principles, for which purpose a statutory instrument is perfectly sufficient. Nonetheless, were a directive to leave open an important point of policy or principle of law, the State would only be able to create such policy by means of an Act of Parliament.

The Supreme Court further clarified this verdict in *Maher v Minister for Agriculture* [2001] 2 I.R. 139, observing that despite the *Meagher* judgment, statutory instruments were not always sufficient for the implementation of EU law. *Maher* concerned the manner of implementation into Irish law of an EC milk quota Regulation. The State decided to implement the EU Regulation by means of a statutory instrument. The plaintiff, who was thus denied his milk quota, argued that the method of implementation contravened Art.15.2. The Supreme Court ruled, however, that in passing this statutory instrument, the Minister was in fact doing no more than giving effect to the principles already contained in the EU measure. "The choices as to policy", Keane C.J. observed, "... have in truth been reduced to vanishing point".

The court clarified, however, that Art.29.4.10 did not of itself justify the use of statutory instruments for the purpose of giving effect to EU law. In sum, a statutory instrument can be used only when the instrument is implementing policies fully contained in the EU measure, and not where the EU measure leaves certain policy decisions to the Member State. In the latter case, an Act of Parliament was necessary in order to create new policy not contained in the EC measure.

Can the Oireachtas give a statutory instrument the same legal force as an Act of Parliament? The Leontjava principle

An interest question arose in the case of *Leontjava and Chang v DPP* [2004] 1 I.R. 591. In the wake of the *Laurentiu* decision noted above, the Immigration Act 1999, s.2, purported to give certain statutory instruments made by the Government on foot of the Aliens Act 1935 the same effect as an Act of Parliament. In other words, the statutory instruments (the "Aliens Order") would have the same standing as Acts of the Oireachtas, though to the extent only that this would be constitutional. The Supreme Court upheld this approach, and concluded that the Oireachtas is entitled to make legislation by reference to material not contained in the body of the Act itself, that is, to incorporate legislation 'by reference'.

No provision of the Constitution expressly prohibits the means of enactment used by the Oireachtas in this case. Thus, the onus of proving such unconstitutionality lay on the person alleging illegality.

The court observed that the sole power of making legislation for the State lies, by virtue of Art.15.2 of the Constitution, with the Oireachtas. The Constitution grants the Oireachtas a wide latitude in adopting whatever legislation it deems appropriate in the circumstances. Where the Oireachtas has clearly and unequivocally stated that a particular instrument should have the force of law in the State, it is entitled to have such an effect. Thus the decision to incorporate the provisions of the Aliens Orders by reference to them rather than by verbatim reproduction of their contents in the Act was a decision that the Oireachtas was entitled to make. The fact that the Act incorporates by reference provisions that have not themselves been enacted in the manner required by Art.25 of the Constitution is not fatal to the validity of the Act.

The Government cannot suspend a law's application by deliberate nonenforcement

A positive decision by the Government *never* to enforce an Act of Parliament that has not yet been terminated by Parliament itself would, according to McCarthy J. in *Norris v Attorney General* [1984] I.R. 36, be unconstitutional. The Government is, after all, not entitled to "repeal" a law, that is, to suspend or terminate its operation, this being within the exclusive powers of the Oireachtas. For instance, in *Hoey v Minister for Justice* [1994] 3 I.R. 329, Lynch J. concluded that it was not possible for a Minister to exempt a local authority from a duty expressly conferred on it by an Act of Parliament.

Example: In *Purcell v The Attorney General* [1995] 3 I.R. 287, a Government decision not to collect any taxes imposed under the Farm Tax Act 1985 was found to be in breach of Art.15.2. As the Act was still in force, the unilateral decision of the Government not to collect these taxes amounted to an unconstitutional attempt to alter the legislative will of the Oireachtas. This reflects the earlier verdict in *Duggan v An Taoiseach* [1989] I.L.R.M. 710, where civil servants in the Farm Tax Office were given damages when they were reassigned to their old jobs, after the Government decided no longer to collect the Farm Tax. As the Act required the collection of the tax, the civil servants had a legitimate expectation that the Act would be enforced unless repealed by the Oireachtas. It could not be repealed by Government action or, for that matter inaction.

The Sheehan principle: delaying the coming into force of legislation

When a piece of legislation is passed by the Oireachtas, and signed by the President, it is quite common to make the coming into force of that legislation conditional upon an Order made by a Government Minister. This is designed to allow the Government time to prepare for the full impact of the Act in question. So, what happens if the Minister refuses to bring the relevant Order into force, or if he otherwise unreasonably delays in putting the Act into operation?

This issue was considered in *State (Sheehan) v Government of Ireland* [1987] I.R. 550. In this case the Oireachtas had enacted s.60 of the Civil Liability Act 1961, changing an old anomaly in the common law of negligence. The Government was empowered by the Act to bring the measure into force as and when it saw fit. Up to the date of the judgment, it had not brought the relevant legislation into force. In 1987, Mr Sheehan unsuccessfully attempted to get the Supreme Court to force the Government to pass the necessary Order. The Supreme Court ruled that the Government was entitled to delay the Order indefinitely, even though this arguably involved the effective reversal of legislative policy. Nonetheless, the court concluded that the Government had a full, unfettered discretion as to when the measure would become operative.

Discussion point: The High Court in *Sheehan*, by contrast, considered that the Government's actions were in breach of the Constitution, Costello J. ruling that the Government could only delay the bringing into force of the legislation for a "reasonable time". Considering that an indefinite delay by the Government effectively frustrated the policy of the Oireachtas, was the Supreme Court wrong in overruling Costello J.?

European Union law

Ireland's membership of the European Union of course qualifies Art.15.2. By virtue of Art.29.4.10° and the European Communities Acts 1972–2007 the Union may make laws that apply in Ireland even where they have not been passed by the Oireachtas. Art.29.4.10° exempts EU law from having to be validated by the Oireachtas and thus allows laws to be created and enforced in Ireland without national parliamentary sanction. (See above in Ch.6).

Parliamentary privilege

Articles 15.10, 15.12 and 15.13 afford certain rights and freedoms to the Houses of Parliament and their members.

Exclusive power of the Houses to regulate their internal operation

Article 15.10 allows each House of Parliament to make and administer its own rules. Where these rules are broken, each House may impose penalties on its members. Furthermore, a decision of either House concerning its internal operation cannot be challenged in any court. In *O'Malley v Ceann Comhairle of the Dáil* [1997] 1 I.R. 427, for instance, the High Court declined to hear a challenge to a decision of the Ceann Comhairle (Speaker of the Dáil) that certain questions could not be asked of a Minister in the Dáil. The courts thus will not generally interfere in the workings of each House. That said, where the operations of the House potentially impinge on the rights of those who are not members of either House, the courts are not so reticent to intervene. In both *Re Haughey* [1971] I.R. 217 and *Maguire v Ardagh* [2002] 2 I.R. 385, the procedures of Oireachtas committees were scrutinized to ensure that the personal rights of non-members were observed.

Article 15.10 also affords to each House a "power" to "protect its official documents and the private papers of its members, and to protect itself and its members against any person or persons interfering with, molesting or attempting to corrupt its members in the exercise of their duties." The nature and extent of this power was considered in *Howlin v Morris* [2004] 2 I.L.R.M. 53, [2006] I.L.R.M. 440. In this case the respondent was the chair of the Morris Tribunal inquiring into allegations of Garda corruption. He sought to compel the plaintiff, a TD, ("Teachta Dála", meaning "a member of the Dáil") to release private papers and telephone records relating to confidential information given to him concerning the corruption allegations. The TD had passed the information on to the Minister for Justice, though it was found that he (the TD) had not relied on the information in utterances before the Dáil. While the Tribunal claimed that it required such information in order to carry out its investigation, the plaintiff asserted that he had received the information in confidence and had a right and duty to preserve that confidentiality. The plaintiff further claimed that such papers were privileged under Art.15.10.

Overturning a High Court decision that the papers were privileged, the Supreme Court noted that Art.15.10 confers a power on each House of the Oireachtas to pass resolutions protecting the private papers of its members. This right, however, was the right of the House, rather than that of individual members. This right, moreover, was not self-executing: it required, rather, a formal enactment of rules by the relevant House, expressly invoking the power and setting out the conditions for the protection of the papers. Neither the Dáil nor the Seanad had enacted such express rules in order to assert this power, and as such, the Deputy's papers were not in fact privileged. In the course of his judgment, Hardiman J. stressed that as the allegations made were very serious, and the good name of citizens was at stake, the Houses of the Oireachtas would only be entitled to withhold their members' papers from a tribunal or court where the relevant House had clearly and expressly invoked the power to do so.

Parliamentary privilege in respect of utterances

Considering the facts in *Howlin*, one must distinguish between a situation where the documents in question led first to utterances before the Dáil, and where they had not. In *Howlin* the court concluded that the papers had not provided the basis for a Dáil statement. It appears, however, that had the papers been relied on in statements made first to either House, the situation may have been radically different, owing to the terms of Arts 15.12 and 15.13.

Articles 15.12 and 15.13 protect every TD and Senator in respect of utterances made in either House. Such utterances are privileged. They also privilege the Official Reports and publications of the Oireachtas or of either House. According to Budd J. in *Blascaod Mór v Commissioners for Public Works* [2001] 1 I.L.R.M. 401, this privilege is designed to safeguard freedom of speech in the Oireachtas.

This means that a Member of Parliament cannot be sued, prosecuted or otherwise brought before a court of law in respect of such comments on the grounds, for instance, that they were defamatory (i.e. libelled or slandered a person), breached confidentiality or incited to hatred contrary to hate speech legislation. This privilege applies to the statement "wherever published", which means that the verbatim republication of the statement by parties outside the House (e.g. in a newspaper or on radio) is also privileged provided, of course, that the statement was first made in the Dáil or the Seanad. The purpose of this measure is to ensure free debate in each of the Houses.

Protecting sources

No TD or Senator can be forced in either a court of law or tribunal to reveal the sources of information used in parliamentary debates. Nor can the Deputy or Senator be penalized in any way for invoking the privilege. In the *Attorney General v Hamilton (No. 2)* [1993] 3 I.R. 227, the Supreme Court ruled that Dáil Deputies who had made allegations in the Dáil based on information from external sources could not be forced to disclose those confidential sources to the Beef Tribunal.

The privilege is restricted to statements made in either House. If a member of either House "voluntarily, consciously and deliberately" repeats the same comments outside the House this would amount to a waiver of their right to immunity, thus removing privilege in respect of those comments. However, in *Hamilton (No. 2)* a majority of the Supreme Court concluded that an elaboration on Dáil statements before the Tribunal (before which the TDs were compelled to testify) did not constitute a waiver of the privilege in respect of the TDs' sources. By the same token, a member of either House cannot confer privilege on himself in respect of a comment first made outside the House, simply by subsequently repeating it in the House.

Privilege from arrest

Article 15.13 prevents the arrest or detention (otherwise than for treason, a felony (an indictable offence), or breach of the peace) of a Member of Parliament in certain circumstances. These circumstances are where the member is going to, is returning from or is within the precincts of either House of the Oireachtas, the purpose again being to ensure that Oireachtas members' right of free speech and the right to vote are not curtailed through arrest. On a strict interpretation, however, this does not necessarily prevent a member from being charged with an offence, provided he is not arrested in or on his way to or from the Oireachtas.

The purpose of parliamentary privilege

The provisions in Arts 15.12 and 15.13 are broadly based on measures found in the Bill of Rights 1689, an agreement between on the one hand, King William III and Queen Mary and on the other hand, the British Parliament. The purpose of the measure was to confirm the rights of Parliament, and to prevent the monarchy from abridging those rights by, for instance, penalizing members in respect of their utterances, or preventing them from attending Parliament, as previous monarchs had done. Some debate arises, however, as to whether this is a right enjoyed by individual members or whether it is properly to be regarded as a right of each House. This is important in determining whether individual members can waive their right to immunity or whether this can only be done with the approval of the House as a whole. To date, the point has not been resolved.

The powers of Oireachtas committees

In the performance of its legislative functions, it is quite common for the Oireachtas and its two constituent Houses to set up committees of members to consider proposals for legislation. On occasion, the Houses have established sub-committees to consider certain matters of public importance. The status of such committees was considered in *Maguire v Ardagh* [2002] 1 I.R. 385. There, the Oireachtas had set up a special sub-committee to inquire into the unfortunate circumstances surrounding the shooting dead of John Carthy in Abbeylara in April 2000. While the sub-committee's findings would have no direct legal effect, there was nonetheless the possibility that a finding of unlawful killing might be made, which might reflect adversely on the Gardaí. Certain members of the Gardaí, having been compelled to attend as witnesses, challenged the constitutional standing of the Committee, arguing that the Oireachtas did not have the power to establish such a committee.

The Supreme Court agreed, concluding that the Oireachtas did not have the inherent general power to set up an investigative committee. While the Oireachtas had limited powers to inquire into certain matters, such powers were limited in the sense that they could only be exercised with a view to assisting in the functions of the House (in particular to make legislation). If the sub-committee were making inquiries with a view to drafting protective legislation, the sub-committee's functioning may have been sound. Here, however, this was not the case. There was no suggestion that the Houses were considering making legislation in the area. The sole purpose of the inquiry was to establish the facts surrounding an admittedly very serious incident. This was beyond the inherent powers of the Oireachtas.

The powers of the Oireachtas did not encompass the power to make findings of fact that could potentially damage the good name of persons who were not members of either House. Although the sub-committee could not penalize a person in respect of any wrongdoing, the findings of the sub-committee as to culpability were nonetheless capable of damaging the good name of a person. Outside the context of its law-making function, the Oireachtas did not have such a general investigative power. In other words, it could not simply take it upon itself to investigate allegations of wrong-doing; it could only do so for specific purposes like helping it to decide how to legislate.

10. THE DÁIL AND THE SEANAD: MAKING LEGISLATION

The Oireachtas consists of the President and two Houses, Dáil Éireann and Seanad Éireann.

The Dáil

The Dáil is the lower House of the Oireachtas. In almost all matters it is more powerful than the Seanad. It currently has 166 members elected from 43 constituencies. There are several important constitutional principles concerning the conduct of a Dáil election (see generally Art.16).

*   Any *citizen of Ireland*, not otherwise disqualified from voting and aged 18 or over, may *vote* in a Dáil election. As a result of the decision of the European Court of Human Rights in *Hirst v United Kingdom (No. 2)* (2006) 42 E.H.R.R. 41 the law has been changed in Ireland to allow prisoners (formerly restricted from voting) to exercise the right to vote.
*   The Constitution (under the Ninth Amendment to the Constitution 1984) also allows voting rights to be given to *non-Irish citizens* resident in Ireland. Under this provision, the right to vote in Dáil elections has been extended to British citizens living in Ireland (on the basis of reciprocal rights being granted to Irish citizens living in Britain).
*   Article 16.2 permits *only Irish citizens aged 21 or over* to run for the Dáil. Certain persons, moreover, *may not run* for the Dáil. These include the President, sitting judges, members of the defence forces and undischarged bankrupts.
*   There may be no more than one TD for every 20,000 of the population but no less than one TD for every 30,000.
*   While absolute equality is not required, representation must be as equal as practicable throughout the State. In *O'Donovan v Attorney General* [1961] I.R. 114, the High Court ruled that Art.16.2 had been breached because the number of TDs per head of population in rural constituencies was significantly greater than that in urban constituencies.

- Constituency boundaries generally must be reconsidered after each census, to ensure equal Dáil representation throughout the State. Failing that, the constituencies must be revised at least once every 12 years. In *O'Malley v An Taoiseach* [1990] I.L.R.M. 461, Hamilton P., while ruling that he could not prevent the President from dissolving the Dáil on the advice of the Taoiseach, agreed that the failure to revise constituency boundaries in light of the 1986 census was unconstitutional. Where the census demonstrates a significant change in the distribution of population, the Oireachtas is obliged to revise the constituencies. In *Murphy and McGrath v Minister for the Environment* [2007] I.E.H.C.185, Clarke J. observed that where census results revealed a clear disparity in the representation of constituencies, there is a duty on the Oireachtas to act urgently to cure the inequality in representation. In that case, however, the judge ruled that it would not have been practically possible for the Oireachtas to act in the very short time between the publication of the 2006 census results and the calling of the 2007 general election.
- Constituencies must consist of no less than *three seats*.
- Voting must proceed by *proportional representation*. Two attempts to remove this requirement, in 1959 and 1968 respectively, were defeated in referendum.
- Voting must proceed by secret ballot. In *McMahon v Attorney General* [1972] I.R. 69, a system whereby fraudulent votes could be traced and identified was declared unconstitutional on the grounds that it infringed the secrecy of the ballot box.

Fairness in the conduct of elections

While the Oireachtas is entitled, under Art.16.7, to regulate the conduct of elections, the courts retain a right to strike down conditions that infringe constitutional rights. In particular the Constitution leans against measures that disproportionately or unfairly undermine or restrict the right to run for election.

- In *Redmond v Minister for the Environment* [2001] 4 I.R. 61, Herbert J. struck down a requirement that any person wishing to run for election had to put down a deposit of IR£300 (€381), only refundable where the candidate received a minimum number of votes. This, the court reasoned, struck unreasonably at the right of citizens to run for election, placing a particularly discriminatory burden on economically disadvantaged candidates.

- In *Cooney, King, Riordan and the Minister for the Environment* [2006] I.E.S.C. 61, the Supreme Court struck down as disproportionate measures that required non-party candidates to be formally nominated in person by 30 electors. The court concluded that the measures adopted were excessively onerous on non-party candidates, and posed a real risk that a candidate might be unfairly barred from election.
- Candidates, parties and groups campaigning in elections and referenda are entitled to be treated equally by the State. It is unconstitutional for the State to favour one candidate, party or campaign over another. See *Kelly v Minister for the Environment* [2002] 4 I.R. 191, *McKenna v An Taoiseach (No. 2)* [1995] 2 I.R. 10, and *Coughlan v Broadcasting Complaints Commission* [2000] 3 I.R. 1, discussed below at pp.129–130.

Nonetheless, the Oireachtas may regulate elections, provided the relevant measures are proportionate and can be justified in the public interest. For instance, in *Ring v Attorney General* [2004] I.R.185, Laffoy J. upheld as constitutional legislation prohibiting one person holding a dual mandate—a county councillor elected to the Dáil was thus required to give up his council seat. The judge reasoned that the objective behind this measure—to strengthen governance at local and national level—supported any restriction on the plaintiff's rights. In particular, she noted that nothing in the proposal prevented County councillors from running for the Dáil. It simply required them, if elected, to choose between one job and the other.

The Seanad

The Seanad (Senate) is the upper House of the Oireachtas. In almost all matters it is less powerful than the Dáil. It has 60 members, elected as follows.

- 43 members are elected by County, City and Borough Councillors, incoming Dáil Deputies and outgoing Senators.
- 11 members are appointed by the Taoiseach first elected after a General Election.
- 6 members are elected by the graduates of the National University of Ireland, and the University of Dublin (Trinity College Dublin) (three from each university).

Because the Taoiseach elected directly after a general election can appoint 11 members to the Seanad, it is very rare that the Government elected by the Dáil will not also have majority support in the Seanad. **Discussion point:** Why should graduates of some but not all third-level institutions be allowed separate representation in the Seanad? Indeed, why should *any* graduate (already well represented in the Dáil) be treated so favourably? **N.B.** While the Seventh Amendment 1979 facilitated the extension of voting rights to graduates of other educational institutions, this extension has yet to occur.

Making legislation

In making legislation, the Dáil is more powerful than the Seanad. Although a Bill may be introduced in either House, no provision of a Bill may become law without Dáil assent. By contrast, a Bill or part of a Bill that is rejected by the Seanad *can* become a law, even in the face of such opposition.

Article 23

Even where the Seanad rejects a Bill proposed by the Dáil, it can nonetheless be passed into law by a resolution of the Dáil. Article 23 allows the Dáil to override the Seanad's rejection of a Bill, although it can only do so after a 90-day delay. Article 23 operates as follows:

- A Bill is introduced in the Dáil and passed by that House.
- The Bill is then sent to the Seanad, which either:
  - rejects the Bill;
  - proposes amendments of which the Dáil does not approve; or
  - neither rejects nor accepts the Bill (i.e. does nothing).
- In such cases, the Bill will be delayed for 90 days, starting on the date that the Bill was first sent to the Seanad.
- After that 90-day period has expired, the Dáil may, within 180 days of that expiry, pass a resolution deeming the Bill to have been passed by both Houses (even in the face of Seanad opposition).

Thus, the Seanad is limited in its powers to reject a Bill that has been passed by Dáil Éireann. The most it can do is delay the Bill for 90 days. (See also the discussion of Art.27 above at pp. 58–59).

"Money Bills"

A "Money Bill" is a Bill proposing the raising of revenue or the expenditure of monies by the State. A good example would be the annual Finance Bill and the Appropriation Bill of each year. Article 22 defines a "Money Bill" as any Bill dealing with, amongst other things:

*   the imposition and collection of taxes
*   the making of public expenditure
*   the creation of a charge on public monies
*   the creation and management of public debts
*   the supply of public monies.

A "Money Bill" may only be initiated in Dáil Éireann. The Seanad, furthermore, is entitled only to make "recommendations" regarding such a Bill, which recommendations the Dáil may safely ignore (Art.21). In addition, if the Seanad does not make recommendations within 21 days, the Bill will be deemed to have passed both Houses at the expiry of that 21 day period. The apparent reason behind these restrictions is that the Dáil, as the directly elected chamber, is considered to be the most appropriate decision-maker in relation to the public finances.

In normal circumstances, the Chairperson of Dáil Éireann decides whether a Bill is or is not a "Money Bill". The Seanad, however, if aggrieved by such a decision, may pass a resolution calling on the President to refer the issue to a "Committee of Privileges". The President may, at her own discretion, decide to do so, but she is not obliged to accede to their request. If she does decide to establish such a committee, it will consist of an equal number of members from each House, with a Supreme Court judge as Chair. This Committee then decides, by majority vote, whether or not the Bill is a "Money Bill". Either way, the Committee's decision is final and conclusive and cannot be challenged in a court of law (Art.22).

The role of Dáil Éireann in declarations of war

Article 28.3.1 stipulates a specific role for the Dáil only in relation to situations of international conflict, stating that "war shall not be declared and the State shall not participate in a war save with the assent of Dáil Éireann". In both *Horgan v Ireland* [2003] 2 I.R. 468 and *Dubsky v Government of Ireland* [2005] I.E.H.C. 442, the plaintiffs challenged the right of the Government to permit stopovers in Shannon airport by US army planes and personnel involved in respectively, the war in Iraq and the war in Afghanistan. Both litigants essentially claimed that this action amounted to a participation in wars without the consent of the Dáil. In *Horgan,* the Dáil had in fact passed a resolution indicating that while the State was not participating in the Iraq conflict, it approved of the provision to the US military of Shannon airport facilities. Noting that the decision of the Government and of the Dáil attracted the presumption of constitutionality, Kearns J. appeared to defer heavily to both bodies in refusing to intervene. The conduct of foreign policy was a matter exclusively reserved to the Government, and the declaration of war a matter solely within the remit of the Dáil. These were matters in which the courts could only interfere where there was an "egregious [outrageously reprehensible] disregard of constitutional rights and duties."

A similar conclusion prevailed in *Dubsky,* Macken J. concluding that the plaintiff had failed to discharge the burden on him of proving that the State was participating in the war in Afghanistan. Reflecting the decision in *Horgan,* the judge again noted that the courts would only intervene in the workings of the Dáil and the Government where the plaintiff could clearly establish a serious breach of the Constitution. For this purpose, the court ruled that the term "war" did not include an armed conflict outside the State in which the State was not a participant.

The balance of power between the Dáil and Seanad

Of the two Houses of the Oireachtas, the Dáil and the Seanad, the Dáil is clearly the more powerful institution, in matters legislative, financial and governmental alike.

In matters legislative the Dáil is clearly the more powerful House. It can veto outright any legislative proposal (or amendments to legislation) put forward by the Seanad. Proposals made by the Dáil, by contrast, can only be delayed by the Seanad and cannot be vetoed. Article 23 permits the Seanad to delay a Bill that it opposes for only 90 days. Once this period expires, the Dáil may pass a resolution deeming the Bill to have been passed by *both* Houses of the Oireachtas. Thus, despite Seanad opposition, the Bill may become law.

In matters financial, moreover, the Seanad has next to no power. The Constitution clearly considers that the directly elected Members of Parliament alone should be allowed to determine the financial policy of the State. It is worth noting that the person holding the office of Minister for Finance can only be drawn from the Dáil and not from the Seanad (Art.28.7). A Bill that is defined as a "Money Bill", furthermore, may only be introduced in the Dáil. (See Art.21). The Seanad may only make recommendations regarding a Money Bill, which recommendations may, furthermore, be ignored by the Dáil.

The Dáil has certain exclusive powers in relation to the operation of the Government. After all, in practice it is the Dáil that selects each new Taoiseach (Art.13.1.1°) and must approve his or her proposed new Government before it may take office. Most of the members of the Government must also be members of the Dáil. While the Taoiseach may appoint Senators to the Government, no more than two Senators may hold ministerial office at any one time. In addition, Senators are not eligible to be appointed as Taoiseach, Tánaiste or Minister for Finance. Each of these roles is reserved to members of the Dáil (see Art.28.7).

The Government, moreover, is generally responsible to the Dáil at all times in respect of its decisions and actions. (Art.28.4). The Government, indeed, depends on the Dáil alone for its continued survival. If the Taoiseach loses the support of a majority of Dáil members, he or she must resign unless the President can be persuaded to dissolve the Dáil (Art.28.10). Where a Taoiseach resigns, the Government as a whole is deemed to have resigned with him or her (Art.28.11). By contrast, a Government may survive for years without the support of a majority of Senators. After all, even if the Seanad rejects a Bill, the Dáil may override its rejection under Art.23. The Seanad, moreover, cannot remove a sitting Taoiseach under any circumstances.

11. THE GOVERNMENT

The Government of the State consists of An Taoiseach (the Prime Minister), An Tánaiste (the Deputy Prime Minister), and a number of other Government Ministers. Article 28.1 allows the Government to have no less than seven members and no more than 15 (including the Taoiseach and Tánaiste). At present, the Government ordinarily consists of 15 members. These persons have "executive responsibility" for the running of the State, in other words they are charged with governing the State on a day-to-day basis. The Government comprises the 'executive branch' of the State, and is often thus termed the "Executive".

The role of the Taoiseach

Appointment of the Taoiseach

The head of the Government is called the Taoiseach, also described in the Constitution as "Prime Minister". The Taoiseach is not directly elected but depends instead on the elected members of the Dáil for his appointment. The President, on the nomination of Dáil Éireann, appoints each new Taoiseach (Art.13.1.1°). In appointing the Taoiseach, the President must effectively act on the instructions of the Dáil, which may only choose a Taoiseach from among its own ranks.

Responsibilities of the Taoiseach

The Taoiseach has overall responsibility for the running of the Government. Beyond this, however, his or her precise role tends to be somewhat vague. In addition to his or her overall brief, the Taoiseach has the following specific duties and powers:

- the nomination of Government Ministers (Art.13.1.2°);
- the power to ask the President to dissolve the Dáil (the President may only refuse to do so when the Taoiseach has lost the support of a majority of Dáil members; Art.13.2.2°);
- the power to appoint 11 members of the Seanad (however, only a Taoiseach first appointed after a general election may do so: Art.18.3);

- the responsibility to inform the President generally concerning matters of national and international policy (Art.28.5.2°);
- the power to nominate the Tánaiste (Art.28.6.1°);
- the power to ask a Minister to resign and, if the request is refused, to demand that resignation (Art.28.9.4°);
- the power to nominate the Attorney General (Art.30.2);
- the Taoiseach is automatically deemed a member of the Council of State, as are all former holders of that office (Art.31); and
- the Taoiseach represents Ireland in the European Council, the body responsible for the overall policy direction of the European Union, and at Intergovernmental Conferences of the EU (when the State holds the Presidency of the Council of Ministers, the Taoiseach becomes the President of the Council of Ministers).

A Taoiseach may, in addition, assign himself or herself a specific ministerial responsibility, although this rarely happens. Charles Haughey was, for instance, Minister for the Gaeltacht from 1987 to 1991.

Resignation of the Taoiseach

Subject to certain conditions, a Taoiseach must resign if he or she loses the support of the majority of the Dáil (Art.28.10). The Taoiseach's resignation has the knock-on effect of terminating the appointments of all the other Government Ministers (Art.28.11). In other words, every Minister depends for his or her continued appointment on the survival of the Taoiseach. That said, the members of the Government (including the Taoiseach) may continue their duties in a care-taking capacity until such time as a new Government is appointed. Similar provisions apply to Ministers in office immediately prior to the dissolution of the Dáil. They continue to hold office until their successors are appointed.

In circumstances where the Taoiseach has lost the support of a majority of Dáil Éireann, he or she normally must resign. The Taoiseach may, however, remain in office if the President, on the Taoiseach's advice, decides to dissolve Dáil Éireann. On such dissolution the Taoiseach and his or her ministers are entitled to remain in office until such time as the Dáil has reassembled after a general election. If at that point the Taoiseach can secure the support of a majority in the Dáil, he or she need not resign at all. If, however, he or she fails to secure such a majority when the Dáil first convenes after the election, the Taoiseach must resign. (Art.28.10)

The "hiring and firing" of Government Members

The appointment of Ministers

Once a new Taoiseach has been appointed, he or she will ask the President to appoint Ministers to the Government (Art.13.1.2°). The Dáil must first approve such Ministers as a group. Only a TD or Senator may be appointed as a member of the Government. That said, the positions of Taoiseach, Tánaiste and Minister for Finance may only be held by members of the Dáil (Art.28.7.1°). Furthermore, no more than two Senators may hold ministerial office at any one time (Art.28.7.2°).

Nonetheless it is at least theoretically possible for an unelected person to be made a Minister. The Taoiseach would first have to appoint such person as one of his or her 11 nominees to the Seanad. Once that has been done, the relevant person could be given a ministerial position, as happened, for instance, to Professor James Dooge, Minister for Foreign Affairs from 1981 to 1982.

Summary: the Ministers of Government

* There should be no less than seven and no more than 15 members of Government, including the Taoiseach.
* Ministers must be members of either the Dáil or the Seanad.
* In particular, the Taoiseach, Tánaiste and Minister for Finance must all be members of the Dáil.
* No more than two Senators at any one time may act as Ministers.
* The Taoiseach may assign Ministers "portfolios", making them responsible for certain tasks or issues, and for Departments of State. The allocation of responsibilities is determined by legislation. The exact confines of each Department and Ministerial position can and do change from time to time, with new Taoisigh often altering the distribution of Ministerial responsibilities.
* Individual Ministers represent Ireland at the EU Council of Ministers.

The removal of Ministers

A Minister may voluntarily resign by handing his resignation to the Taoiseach. This is then delivered to the President who, with the consent of the Taoiseach, terminates the Minister's term of office (Art.28.9.3°). The Taoiseach is also entitled to ask a Minister to resign

for any reason that, to the Taoiseach, appears sufficient. If the Minister
fails to accede to this request, the Taoiseach is empowered to order
that the President terminate the appointment of that Minister
(Art.28.9.4°). This happened in 1990, when the then Taoiseach Charles
Haughey, under pressure from his cabinet colleagues, sacked Minister
Brian Lenihan Sr. following unproven allegations that the latter had
sought to persuade the President not to dissolve the Dáil in 1982.

Executive privilege

Prior to 1972, it was widely believed that the Government enjoyed
what was called the "executive privilege". This privilege allowed the
Government to refuse to disclose the content of (or even sometimes
the very *existence* of) documents relating to the operation of
Government. This was a royal prerogative right enjoyed by the King
or Queen of England. It was wrongly believed that the executive in
Ireland had inherited this right to refuse court access to its documents.
(See also *Byrne v Ireland*, discussed above in Ch.5.)

In *Murphy v Dublin Corporation* [1972] I.R. 215, the Supreme
Court struck down the executive privilege as being inconsistent with
the Constitution. The privilege, the court held, infringed the court's
right and duty to consider all relevant evidence in a case before it. The
lack of access to certain evidence, in other words, potentially
undermined its ability to achieve justice in a particular case.

Thus, whether such documents should be withheld in appropriate
cases was a decision solely for the court to make, not the Government.
There was, furthermore, no class of documents that could generally be
excluded from court scrutiny. Judges had to decide on a case-by-case
basis whether certain documents should be withheld or not. This case,
thus, effectively restored to the courts the right to determine whether
Government documents should be admitted as evidence. As such, it is
an important illustration of how the separation of powers operates
between the executive and the courts.

Cabinet confidentiality

Notwithstanding the decision in *Murphy*, discussions between
Government members around the cabinet table are privileged, that is
to say they must be kept confidential, even from a court of law. The
Government is said to have "collective responsibility" for its actions
(Art.28.4.2°). This means that it must think and act as one body. Each

Minister, thus, takes personal responsibility for the decisions of the Government as a whole. If Ministers, thus, were able to reveal disagreements or conflicts in the cabinet, it is thought that the collective responsibility of Government might thereby be undermined.

Attorney General v Hamilton (No. 1)

The principle of cabinet confidentiality was confirmed in *Attorney General v Hamilton (No. 1)* [1993] 2 I.R. 250). In this case, the Beef Tribunal (inquiring into certain irregularities in the beef industry) had been questioning a Minister regarding his recollections of a cabinet meeting. In the course of this line of questioning, the Attorney General interjected, alleging that the rule regarding cabinet confidentiality prevented the Minister from divulging such information.

While the High Court (O'Hanlon J.) rejected this proposition, the Supreme Court on appeal ultimately affirmed the view of the Attorney General. It ruled that discussions at the cabinet table between members of Government could not be divulged, even before a tribunal of inquiry. The majority's reasoning was that to allow disagreements and differences of opinion to be exposed outside the cabinet room would undermine the collective responsibility and authority of the Government. The court also reasoned that by rendering cabinet discussions confidential, Government Ministers would be encouraged to give frank opinions on matters that were sensitive or controversial.

This case had a number of important consequences:

*   Government Ministers could not be questioned regarding the details of cabinet discussions, even before a court or tribunal;
*   Government Ministers were precluded from revealing the substance of such discussions, even if they wanted to do so;
*   Courts and tribunals were precluded from obtaining pertinent evidence where such evidence comprised of discussions at the cabinet table, or where it related to documents prepared for or discussed at such meetings.

It is important to note that cabinet confidentiality is a collective right of the Government rather than any individual minister's right. An individual minister cannot, even after he or she leaves office, waive such confidentiality. In other words, cabinet confidentiality imposes a duty on ministers, not a right.

The Seventeenth Amendment

To remedy the rigidity of this rule, the People amended the Constitution in 1997, adding the Seventeenth Amendment of the Constitution. The Seventeenth Amendment (inserting a new Art.28.4.3°) affirms the principle of cabinet confidentiality. It introduces, however, two important exceptions to its operation. Although the principle of cabinet confidentiality remains largely intact, the High Court may lift the requirement of cabinet confidentiality in two cases:

• On application by a tribunal of inquiry seeking information concerning cabinet discussions. Such an application may be granted only if it is established that there is "an overriding public interest" in such disclosure. This provision applies only to a tribunal established by the Government under authorisation from the Oireachtas.

• On application by any court of law, where such disclosure is shown to be in the "interests of the administration of justice".

Discussion point: Did the Seventeenth Amendment go far enough? Is the cabinet confidentiality rule still too restrictive? Would it change that much if we knew what Government Ministers *really* thought?

12. THE ATTORNEY GENERAL

The Attorney General occupies two unusually conflicting roles. On the one hand, the holder of this post is the chief legal adviser to the Government. Although he is not a member of the Government, the Attorney General is effectively hired and fired by the Taoiseach. Yet the Attorney General is also charged with protecting and vindicating the public interest, a role that potentially brings him into conflict with the Government he serves.

Who appoints the Attorney General?

On the nomination of the Taoiseach, the President appoints the Attorney General, although it is effectively the Taoiseach who decides on the occupant of the post. While the Attorney General cannot be a member of the Government (Art.30.4) his continued occupancy of this role depends in essence on the continued approval of the Taoiseach. Just as the Taoiseach chooses the Attorney General, so too can the former demand the Attorney's resignation. If the Attorney General should refuse this request, the President shall terminate his appointment.

The role of the Attorney General

Article 30 specifically refers only to the Attorney General's role as legal adviser to the Government. Section 6 of the Ministers and Secretaries Act 1924, in more extensive terms, charges the Attorney with the oversight of "... the representation of the Government ... and of the public in all legal proceedings for the enforcement of law, the punishment of offenders and the assertion or protection of public rights ...". The Attorney bears the duty to advise the Government and Ministers in matters of law and of legal opinion. The Attorney, additionally, is allocated certain specific functions by legislation, one of which is to pre-approve certain extradition applications.

Independence of the role

Despite his dependency on the Taoiseach's continued favour, the courts have clearly asserted that the Attorney General is independent of Government. In *McLoughlin v Minister for Social Welfare* [1958] I.R. 1 the Supreme Court concluded that an employee of the Chief

State Solicitor's Office, which in turn answers to the Attorney General's Office, was not a 'government' employee for the purposes of social welfare law. The Attorney General is "independent" of (and not an arm of) Government. As such, the plaintiff was not an employee of the Government.

In the course of his judgment, Kingsmill Moore J. observed that the Attorney General was not a servant of the Government but rather an independent Constitutional Officer. This was underlined by the fact that the Constitution provided for the forced or voluntary resignation of the Attorney, acknowledging that the Attorney may be required in certain circumstances to pursue proceedings in the face of Government opposition.

Indeed, the Attorney General is entitled, in his own right, to take steps to uphold the Constitution and the law even where the Government opposes such action. In *Attorney General v X* [1992] 1 I.R. 1, the Attorney General took proceedings to restrain a 14-year-old girl from going to the UK to obtain an abortion. It is more than likely that at least some members of the Government opposed these steps. Notwithstanding such disapproval and the eventual failure of the Attorney's case, the Supreme Court expressly agreed that the Attorney was well within his rights to take such a case.

Prosecution of offences

Article 30.3 states that all non-summary crimes and offences should be prosecuted in the name of the People. The Article applies to prosecutions other than those taken in a court responsible for trying only minor offences (generally the District Court).

It was originally envisaged that the Attorney General would be primarily responsible for the taking of non-summary prosecutions. The Constitution, however, provides that "some other person authorised in accordance with law" may act instead of the Attorney. Due to the heavy workload of the Attorney General, the Prosecution of Offences Act 1974 created a new office of Director of Public Prosecutions (DPP) with responsibility for taking prosecutions against alleged offenders. Nowadays, as a result, most non-summary prosecutions are taken by the DPP, although the Attorney General retains the sole power to instigate certain types of prosecution, for instance for genocide.

The DPP retains the independence enjoyed by the Attorney General in respect of such offences. Thus the courts cannot generally review a decision of the DPP unless it can be shown that the DPP acted in bad faith or in pursuance of an improper motive. In *H. v DPP* [1994] 2 I.L.R.M. 285, for instance, the High Court refused to hear a review of the DPP's decision not to prosecute a person in respect of the alleged sexual abuse of a minor. Prior to 1974, the Attorney General enjoyed a similarly unrestricted discretion. In *State (Killian) v Attorney General* (1958) 92 I.L.T.R. 182 the Supreme Court ruled that the Attorney General could not be forced by the courts to take a prosecution. In that case a convicted prisoner alleged that another person had in fact committed the offence for which the prisoner had been incarcerated. The Attorney General, however, refused to reopen the case. The court noted that the decision to prosecute was solely one for the Attorney to make.

In *Norris v Attorney General* [1984] I.R. 36, however, McCarthy J. warned that a policy decision *never* to prosecute a particular offence (in this case the former crimes of buggery and gross indecency between males) would be unconstitutional. The DPP (and by implication the Attorney General) in other words are obliged to obey and enforce the law. While the DPP may, of course, decide that a prosecution is not appropriate in a particular case, the Constitution precludes him (or anyone else for that matter) from making a positive decision generally to refrain from enforcing the law in all cases of a particular offence. To permit the DPP to do so, McCarthy J. pointed out, would involve allowing him to alter the law of the State, a task reserved by Art.15 to the Oireachtas. (See above at pp.62–63).

The Attorney General as defender of public rights

In addition to his role advising the Government, the Attorney General is also charged with ensuring compliance with the Constitution. Section 6 of the Ministers and Secretaries Act 1924 makes the Attorney responsible for "the assertion or protection of public rights". To this end the Attorney General may take a case seeking to have the law (including, in particular, the Constitution) enforced. For instance, in the *Attorney General v X.* [1992] 1 I.R. 1, the then Attorney General sought an injunction to prevent a 14-year-old girl from travelling to Britain for an abortion. The Attorney General believed that this was necessary to defend the right to life of an unborn child. The Supreme Court ultimately ruled that, in the particular circumstances of that case, such an injunction should not be granted. It nevertheless expressly noted that the Attorney General had acted properly at all times to vindicate the rights of the unborn child, as was his right and duty under the Constitution. In *Attorney General v Hamilton (No. 1)* [1993] 2 I.R. 250, the Attorney General again took an action seeking this time to enforce the constitutional principle of cabinet confidentiality. (See above at pp.66–68).

In taking such actions the Attorney General may of course find himself in conflict with the wishes of the Government. This is an aspect of the Attorney General's independence—his responsibility in upholding the public interest may bring him into conflict with the Taoiseach who appointed him. Notably, the Taoiseach may demand the removal of an Attorney General for any reason, including the fact that the Attorney General has sought to pursue a course of legal action of which the Government disapproves.

The right to take a case asserting the public interest or attempting to enforce the law, however, is not reserved exclusively to the Attorney General. Any person who is personally affected by an alleged breach of the law or the Constitution (i.e. with locus standi) may take such a case. It is possible also for a concerned individual with a genuine, bona fide interest in the upholding of the law or Constitution to take such a case. (See further the discussion above at pp.22-23). After all, every citizen has an interest in seeing that the Constitution is upheld. This right is all the more important considering that the Attorney General, being an adviser to the Government, is in reality more likely to be predisposed to the view of the Government than the average citizen.

13. THE COURTS

The Constitution provides for a system of courts presided over by judges. These courts have the sole and exclusive power (subject to Art.37) to administer justice, that is, broadly speaking, to determine legal disputes.

A brief summary of the courts and their functionaries

Courts

- The *Supreme Court* is the highest court in the land. It operates almost exclusively as an appeal court, hearing appeals from cases in lower courts. In fact, it only has "original jurisdiction", that is, the exclusive right to hear a case not previously considered by a court, in two specified situations. These exceptions are laid out in Art.12.3 (the power to determine the incapacity of the President) and Art.26 (the power to review the constitutionality of Bills before they become law).
- The Supreme Court has eight judges: a Chief Justice and seven ordinary justices. Additionally, the President of the High Court is a member also of the Supreme Court and may hear cases before that court. The court sits in chambers of three, five, or (very occasionally) seven judges. In cases concerning the constitutionality of a Bill under Art.26, at least five judges must be present.
- The *High Court* is the main court of first instance. It has full original jurisdiction to determine all judicial matters, whether of law or fact, civil or criminal (Art.34.3). In particular, the constitutionality of a law may only be challenged in the High Court, and not in any other court, subject to the prospect of an appeal to the Supreme Court. (See *People (DPP) v S.M.* [2003] 1 I.R. 606).
  - Every decision of the High Court on a matter of constitutional law may, without exception, be appealed to the Supreme Court. (Art.34.4.4)
  - Every other decision of the High Court may, unless legislation provides otherwise, be appealed to the Supreme Court. (Art.34.4.3)

Article 34.3.4° allows for the creation of courts of local or limited jurisdiction. The two main courts in this category are the Circuit Court and the District Court.

- The *Circuit Court* can try most forms of serious crime involving a jury trial. It may also hear civil cases involving sums of no more than €38,092. In addition, most major family law cases (for instance, divorce proceedings) are heard in this court.
- The *District Court's* criminal jurisdiction extends only to "minor" offences, not requiring a trial by jury. Its civil remit is limited to minor family law cases, and cases that involve sums not exceeding €6,348.

Legislation also provides for the establishment of the Small Claims Court and a Court of Criminal Appeal. The Constitution itself, however, also provides for the existence of a Special Criminal Court. Article 38.3 allows for the establishment of Special Courts for the trial of offences. The key feature of these courts is that instead of a jury, the accused is tried before three judges drawn from the ordinary courts of the State. This means that an accused is effectively deprived, in such cases, of his usual right to a trial by jury. This may only be done where "... the ordinary courts are deemed inadequate to secure the effective administration of justice and the preservation of public peace and order".

Judges

Judges are formally appointed by the President under Art.35.1. In fact, all of these appointments are made on the instructions of the Government, which in turn generally follows the recommendations of the independent Judicial Appointments Advisory Board. To be eligible to serve as a judge, one must usually have served as a practising solicitor or barrister for a minimum period of time.

Article 35.5 stipulates that, during the course of his office, a judge's salary cannot be reduced. Such an unconstitutional reduction might arise, for instance, if the State failed to raise judicial salaries in response to significant levels of inflation (see O'Flaherty J. in *McMenamin v Ireland* [1996] 3 I.R. 100). The imposition of ordinary taxes on a judge's salary, however, does not constitute a reduction for these purposes (see *O'Byrne v Minister for Finance* [1959] I.R. 1).

Judicial impartiality

When being invested as a judge, the person in question must take the oath of office laid out in Art.34.5, promising in particular to perform his or her duties "without fear or favour, affection or ill-will" towards any person. Judges, moreover, cannot simultaneously hold down any other office or paid position, including membership of either House of the Oireachtas.

Example: In *Dublin Wellwoman Centre v Ireland* [1995] 1 I.L.R.M. 408, the late Carroll J. was prevented from hearing a case relating to the right to distribute information on abortion. This was because Carroll J., as Chairperson of the Commission on the Status of Women, had made certain public representations concerning this very issue. While the Supreme Court agreed that there was no doubt that the Judge herself would act completely impartially in this case, it pointed out there was a reasonable *perception* of bias that precluded the Judge from hearing the case.

The independence of the judiciary

Article 35.2 guarantees the independence of the judiciary, subject only to the Constitution and the law.

Example: *Buckley v Attorney General* [1950] I.R. 67 concerned the ownership of funds held in the name of "Sinn Féin". The ownership of the money being in dispute, proceedings were taken in the High Court to decide which of a number of parties was entitled to the money. While these proceedings were ongoing, that is, while the judge was considering this case, the Oireachtas passed the Sinn Féin Funds Act 1947. This Act purported to end the case and distribute the money involved between survivors of the War of Independence.

The Supreme Court ruled that this Act was unconstitutional. Once a case has commenced in the courts, only the courts can decide the outcome of the case. In other words, the Oireachtas cannot tell the court how to do its job. The Oireachtas's intervention in this case amounted to a breach of the separation of powers and an interference with the independence of the judiciary.

Murphy v British Broadcasting Corporation [2004] I.E.H.C. 440 stresses another aspect of the independence of the judiciary. There, McKechnie J. concluded (despite the right to a jury secured by Art.38.5) that contempt of court, even where non-minor, did not ordinarily require a trial by jury (though some limited exceptions applied, where the matter was criminal, non-minor and the facts were in contention). He stressed that the conduct of court cases was a matter exclusively reserved to the judiciary, who were deemed independent in the performance of this function. This independence could not be maintained, he observed, if the courts "could not master their own destiny". The courts thus were entitled to protect their integrity and dignity against unjust comment, a power that would have been undermined if they had to "... cede any part of [this] self-protecting obligation to a jury".

Once a case has been decided, the Oireachtas cannot overturn the decision

It is of course possible for the Oireachtas to change the law so as to ensure that the result of future cases may be different from those that have gone before. In doing so, however, the Oireachtas has to be careful not to attempt to deny the victors in cases already decided of the benefit of court decisions in their favour.

Example: In *Howard v Commissioners of Public Works* [1994] 1 I.R. 101, the High Court ruled that an interpretative centre being built by the State without the required planning permission did in fact require such permission. (The Supreme Court later confirmed this decision). Immediately after the High Court decision, the Oireachtas changed the law to exempt (with retrospective effect) all State buildings from the need to obtain planning permission. The legislation was framed, however, to leave intact the specific outcome in *Howard*. That case having decided that the interpretative centre in question could not be built without planning permission, the legislation would have been unconstitutional had it attempted to reverse the specific decision of the court in that case, depriving the plaintiffs of their judicial victory. The legislation was found to be constitutionally valid, but only because it had not attempted to disturb the specific outcome of the *Howard* litigation. (See *Howard v Commissioners for Public Works (No. 3)* [1994] 3 I.R. 394).

Example: In *Pine Valley v Minister for the Environment* [1987] I.R. 23, the plaintiff had obtained outline planning permission from the Minister for Local Government for the construction of a building. The High Court subsequently ruled that such permission was invalid as it infringed the county development plan for the relevant area. Nevertheless, the Oireachtas subsequently passed legislation exempting an outline planning permission from being declared invalid by reason only of the fact that it infringed a local development plan. Although the legislation operated with retrospective effect, it expressly excluded from its remit (i.e. it did *not* exempt) any outline planning permission that had been the subject of a court case.

This meant, thus, that the plaintiff remained without outline planning permission. Although the court in this case agreed that such treatment was discriminatory (and possibly in breach of Art.40.1), it ultimately concluded that the discrimination was justified by the need to safeguard the integrity of judicial decisions. The legislature, in short, could not reverse the outcome of this specific court case.

Removal of judges from office

In the ordinary course of events, a judge will serve as such until he or she retires. As a consequence of the independence of the judiciary, a judge once appointed cannot normally be removed from office. In particular, a judge cannot be sacked for issuing a judgment considered unfavourable to the Government or Oireachtas.

Article 35.4.1, however, allows a High Court or Supreme Court judge to be removed from office where the judge has behaved inappropriately or, in the alternative, has become incapacitated. The Article confers on the Oireachtas a power to 'impeach' a judge, that is, to remove him or her from office. This may only be done, however, "... for stated misbehaviour or incapacity, and then only upon resolutions passed by Dáil Éireann and Seanad Éireann calling for his removal."

By contrast with Art.12.10, which lays down a relatively detailed process for the impeachment of the President, Art.35.4 is vague on the precise procedures to be applied in impeaching a judge. Nor is any guidance offered on the meaning of "misbehaviour" for this purpose, the point presumably being for the Oireachtas to determine in each case.

In *Curtin v Dáil Éireann* [2006] I.E.S.C. 14, the Supreme Court offered some clarification on the appropriate process. This case concerned the proposed impeachment of Judge Brian Curtin. (Although Judge Curtin was a Circuit Court judge, it was accepted that the terms of Art.35.4 applied equally to him, given the fact that the tenure of such judges is the same as that of a High Court judge.) Judge Curtin had previously been charged with downloading child pornography onto a computer, but had been acquitted on the direction of the trial judge presiding in the case. Despite the acquittal, the

Oireachtas decided formally to investigate the judge's alleged conduct in order to decide whether he should be removed from office.

Judge Curtin unsuccessfully challenged the procedures set out by the Oireachtas for this purpose. The process adopted by the Oireachtas required a joint select committee to gather evidence, which would be presented to each House. On foot of that evidence, each House would then consider separately a resolution to remove the judge from office. The procedures adopted by the Oireachtas allowed the committee to compel the attendance of judges to give evidence, and to require the submission of documentation to the committee.

Judge Curtin claimed first, that the impeachment procedure adopted by the Houses was not permitted by the Constitution. In the High Court, Smyth J. rejected the proposition that, as in the case of the President, the charge should have been made by one House and considered in a trial before the other House of the Oireachtas. The Constitution was clear that a resolution of each House was required, and that the misbehaviour must be identified in that resolution. Beyond that, Art.35.4 was silent on the specific procedures to be adopted, but given that the Constitution conferred this task on the Oireachtas, it was open to the Oireachtas to determine the manner in which the impeachment process proceeded.

The Supreme Court agreed. It noted first that the resolutions of the Oireachtas enjoyed the presumption of constitutionality. It was presumed, furthermore, that the Oireachtas would act in line with fair procedures. Turning to the actual process adopted by the Oireachtas, although the Supreme Court agreed that a different process might well have been preferable, it concluded that it was open to the Oireachtas to select the procedure for impeachment that they had chosen in this case. Noting the doctrine of the separation of powers, the courts would only interfere where there was a clear disregard of constitutional principles, which had not occurred in this case.

Nonetheless, considerations of fairness as well as a close reading of the Article required that, before the Houses decided whether or not to remove the judge, "the Appellant should be entitled to a distinct hearing and decision on the facts ...". The court observed that the wording of Art.35.4 required first that there be a determination of "stated misbehaviour" and only then separate resolutions for impeachment.

The Supreme Court also rejected Judge Curtin's proposition that the sub-committee's power to compel him to give evidence infringed the independence of the judiciary. While judges normally are not answerable to the Oireachtas, Art.35.4 necessarily required that in order to carry out its function, the Oireachtas needed to be able to ask the Judge relevant questions.

Finally, both courts rejected the claim that because the computer at the centre of the allegations had earlier been unlawfully seized (and thus excluded from consideration in the criminal trial) the Oireachtas had no power to compel its presentation to the committee. Legislation permitted the Oireachtas lawfully to require the production of the computer. The fact that it had been unlawfully seized in the past did not prevent it from being lawfully produced to the committee in the future.

Justice to be administered in public

Article 34.1 requires that, subject to limited exceptions, justice be administered in public. This means that (even if no members of the public are in fact in attendance) members of the public have a constitutional right to attend court proceedings. The courts have observed that an aspect of this right of publicity necessarily involves permitting contemporaneous reports of court proceedings in the media. (See, for instance, *Irish Times v Ireland* [1998] 1 I.R. 359 and *Sutter v Switzerland* (1984) 6 E.H.R.R. 272).

Two reasons may be offered for this rule:

- The courts (per Walsh J. in *Re R. Ltd.* [1989] I.R. 126) are administering justice "on behalf of the inhabitants of the State". Members of the public have a right to know what their courts are doing on their behalf, and to see that the Constitution and the law are being observed. This ensures that there can be confidence in the administration of justice.
- More urgently, the prospect that an accused person might be unfairly treated is heightened if he or she is tried behind closed doors. Such injustice is less likely where justice is administered in the glaring light of publicity. It is important that the public perceives judges to be fair and impartial, that justice not only is done but is seen to be done. Where decisions are made in secret, it is easy for the perception of unfairness, whether this perception is justified or not, to flourish.

Legitimate restrictions on publicity

The rule regarding publicity is not absolute but may be limited in "such special and limited cases as may be prescribed by law". For instance, specific legislation restricts full public access to the courts in cases involving marital breakdown and child custody, the commission of sexual offences (in particular, though not exclusively, against a minor, the purpose being to protect the victim), the care of children, and the protection of trade and business secrets. In the main, such restrictions are permitted where necessary to uphold other constitutional rights or legitimate interests.

As a general rule, such restrictions must be set out in legislation. The courts, however, have an inherent jurisdiction, in the absence of legislation, to restrict publicity. They may do so in order to preserve the constitutional rights of others, most notably the right of an accused to a fair trial. This power must, however, be exercised sparingly. In *Irish Times v Ireland* [1998] 1 I.R. 359 the Supreme Court agreed that the right to a fair trial took precedence over the requirement of publicity in Art.34.1. However, in that case the court concluded that a ban on contemporaneous reporting of a specific trial was not justified. Restrictions could only be applied where there was a real risk of an unfair trial that could not be alleviated by directions to the jury. In this case, there was insufficient evidence of a risk significant enough to justify restrictions on what the courts assumed would be accurate reporting of the trial. See also *Foley v Sunday Newspapers* [2005] 1 I.R. 89 and *Independent Newspapers v Anderson* [2006] I.E.H.C. 62.

Defining the judicial role

In several cases the courts have had to consider the meaning of the "administration of justice" or the "judicial role" reserved to the courts by Art.34.1 of the Constitution. What then is the judicial role?

> An administration of justice or the judicial role basically presupposes a power to determine (decide) a dispute concerning the existence of legal rights and liabilities or the imposition of legal penalties.

In *McDonald v Bord na gCon (No. 2)* [1965] I.R. 217, Kenny J. identified five characteristic features of a judicial function:

- it involves a dispute or controversy as to the existence of legal rights or as to a violation of the law;
- it results in a determination or decision as to the existence of legal rights or obligations, the imposition of legal liability, or the infliction of a legal penalty;
- the determination of the court is final (though in most cases subject to appeal) as regards the presence of legal rights or liabilities or as regards the imposition of a penalty;
- the State is obliged to enforce those rights, liabilities and penalties; and
- the function is one that has traditionally been performed by courts in this country.

The following are some examples of functions that have been determined to be judicial functions:

- the determination of the guilt or innocence of a person in a criminal trial;
- the imposition of a sentence upon conviction.

The determination of the guilt or innocence of a person in a criminal trial

Only a court (usually a jury) may decide that a person is guilty or not guilty of a crime.

Example: In *Re Haughey* [1971] I.R. 217, the Supreme Court determined that an Oireachtas Committee could not "try and convict" a person (not being a member of the Oireachtas itself) who had refused to give evidence before the Committee. Although the Committee could refer the matter to the High Court, the Committee itself was not empowered to determine the guilt of the accused.

The imposition of a sentence upon conviction

Where a person has been convicted of a crime, only a court can decide that person's punishment.

Example: In *Deaton v Attorney General* [1963] I.R. 170, the Supreme Court ruled that a law that gave the Revenue Commissioners the power to decide the penalties to be imposed on those convicted of customs offences was unconstitutional. Only a court, it said, could impose such a penalty.

Example: In *State (Sheerin) v Kennedy* [1966] I.R. 379, a power given to the Minister for Justice to add "hard labour" to a juvenile convict's sentence was deemed to amount to a breach of the judiciary's exclusive powers to determine the punishment of offenders.

Example: In *State (O.) v O'Brien* [1973] I.R. 50, the High Court ruled that a provision that allowed the Minister for Justice to detain a convicted juvenile indefinitely (i.e. with no certain date for release), was unconstitutional on two counts. First, the Minister was not entitled to determine the sentence of a convicted person. Second, the sentence of a prisoner must be of a definite duration.

But see: In *Re Gallagher* [1991] 1 I.R. 31, however, the Supreme Court ruled that an accused person could be detained at the pleasure of the Government where he had been found "guilty but insane". Such a verdict technically amounts to a verdict of acquittal; indeed, nowadays the appropriate verdict would be "not guilty by reason of insanity". As such there is no "punishment" to be handed down. Instead, the acquitted party is placed in the care of the Executive, which must decide when he or she is cured sufficiently of his or her mental illness.

The effect of Article 13.6

Neither the Government nor the legislature may impose a penalty on a particular offender or increase the harshness of an already existing criminal penalty. That said, it is open to the Minister for Justice, under s.23 of the Criminal Justice Act 1951, to shorten ("commute") a punishment or replace it with a lesser punishment ("remit" such punishment). These powers were originally vested in the President under Art.13.6. That Article, however, permitted these powers to be transferred by law to other officials.

Maximum and mandatory penalties

It is important in this context to distinguish between:

- setting the range of penalties generally open to a judge when a crime has been committed; and
- imposing a particular penalty in a specific case of criminal wrongdoing.

In *Deaton,* the Supreme Court made it clear that while only judges may determine what sentence a particular offender must serve in the case of a specific crime, it is within the powers of the Oireachtas generally to prescribe minimum and maximum penalties for certain offences. This view was endorsed by the Supreme Court in *Osmanovic v DPP* [2006] I.E.S.C. 50, the court holding that the Oireachtas has the power to set out the general parameters within which the courts may impose sentences. The Oireachtas is, in other words, entitled to indicate to the courts the range of penalties that will be open to them where a particular crime has been committed. While the courts decide what specific sentence should be imposed depending on the facts of a particular case, the Oireachtas is well within its rights to indicate generally the severity of penalties for particular types of crime. In summary, while only the courts may choose the particular sentence for a particular offender, the Oireachtas can choose the appropriate range of penalties for a particular *offence.*

It seems that even the imposition by Parliament of a mandatory penalty (as with murder), where one set penalty is fixed by legislation, is not unconstitutional. In *State (O'Rourke) v Kelly* [1983] I.R. 58, for instance, the Supreme Court indicated that setting a mandatory penalty would be "within the competence of the Oireachtas". Likewise, in *Deaton*, Ó Dálaigh C.J. distinguished between setting a fixed penalty for an offence, which the Oireachtas may do, and selecting a penalty in a particular case, which only a judge may do. Where a range of penalties was available, only a court may select the particular penalty. This, however, did not prevent the Oireachtas from setting a single, fixed penalty in cases where a person was convicted of a crime. According to the Supreme Court in *Deaton*, a mandatory single or fixed penalty may be set by the Oireachtas. This view was confirmed in *Whelan and Lynch v Minister for Justice, Equality and Law Reform* unreported, High Court, Irvine J., October 5, 2007, where Irvine J. rejected the contention that the mandatory life sentence for murder infringed the Constitutional separation of powers. The judge concluded that the Legislature was entitled to set a mandatory penalty, provided it was proportionate to do so.

Matters of discipline

In other cases, the law remains somewhat uncertain as to whether particular functions amount to judicial functions.

In *Re the Solicitors' Act 1954* [1960] I.R. 239, the Supreme Court ruled that a decision to strike practitioners from the roll of solicitors was a judicial function. The crucial factor in this decision was that the function was traditionally one carried out by the Chief Justice, the solicitor being, historically, an officer of the court. It involved also the "imposition of a penalty", which one judge (rather melodramatically) likened to a severe prison sentence.

The authority of the *Solicitors'* case has since been doubted, with judges and lawyers alike tending to confine its influence to the specific facts of the case. Nonetheless, the fear that disciplinary procedures may be struck down as an invasion of judicial functions has led the Oireachtas to require that certain decisions to dismiss a practitioner be endorsed by (or at least subject to cancellation by) a High Court judge (e.g. Medical Practitioners Act 1978, Dentists Act 1985, Nurses Act 1985).

That said, the better view may be that employment-related disciplinary procedures are not part of the "judicial function" and that the *Solicitors'* case was so decided only because of the historical role of solicitors in the work of the courts. For example, in *Keady v Garda Commissioner* [1992] 2 I.R. 197, the Supreme Court concluded that the dismissal of a Garda for misbehaviour was not a judicial function and could, thus, quite constitutionally be carried out by the defendant Garda Commissioner.

Matters of internal prison discipline, it seems, may also be dealt with without recourse to the courts. This is so even where the breach of discipline, if proved, would also amount to a crime. In *State (Murray) v McRann* [1979] I.R. 133, a prisoner was alleged to have assaulted a prison officer. The governor of the prison, having investigated the matter, ruled that she should forfeit certain privileges normally extended to prisoners. The High Court rejected the prisoner's assertion that this amounted to the exercise of a judicial function. The prison governor was simply acting so as to maintain internal prison discipline and this was not a judicial matter. The fact that the alleged act might also have been prosecuted as a crime was irrelevant. (Similar principles would apply to matters of internal school discipline.)

Other functions

In some cases, the courts have definitively found that certain activities do not involve a judicial function.

Even though it may be presided over by a judge, a tribunal of inquiry is not a court. It thus has no power to carry out any judicial functions. The sole function of a tribunal, according to the Supreme Court in *Goodman International v Hamilton (No. 1)* [1992] 2 I.R. 542, is to determine certain facts and to report those facts to the Oireachtas.

This does not, the court concluded, impinge upon any judicial function. It is no part of the tribunal's role to resolve legal disputes, determine legal liability or impose penalties on errant parties on the basis of its findings of fact or otherwise. As a result, the Supreme Court held that the Beef Tribunal, as a body merely charged with the finding of facts and no more, was not performing a judicial function.

In *Kennedy v Hearne* [1988] I.R. 481, the Supreme Court ruled that the Revenue Commissioners were not administering justice in assessing the tax liability of employers who fail to deduct tax from their employees' wages. In doing so the Revenue Commissioners were not determining a legal dispute between parties, nor were they performing a function traditionally reserved to judges.

Article 37

The purpose and effect of Art.37 often confuses students and should thus be studied with care. Article 37 operates to allow certain limited types of judicial function to be performed by bodies other than courts. There are two basic requirements in Art.37:

• the function must not relate to "criminal matters";
• the function must be limited in terms of its impact.

By "limited" it is meant that the effects of the exercise of such a function should not be unduly serious in their impact. A non-limited power is one that (according to the Supreme Court in *Re the Solicitors' Act 1954* [1960] I.R. 239):

"... is calculated ordinarily to affect in the most profound and far-reaching way the lives, liberties, fortunes and reputations of those against whom [it is] exercised ..."

Example: In *Re the Solicitors' Act 1954* [1960] I.R. 239, the Supreme Court struck down a law allowing the Law Society of Ireland to strike a person off the roll of solicitors. This was, the court agreed, a judicial function. Article 37 could not apply to the Act, moreover, because of the serious effects of the decisions of the Law Society (namely, depriving a person of their livelihood and profession).

Example: By contrast, in *Central Dublin Development Association v Attorney General* (1975) 109 I.L.T.R. 69 a judicial function performed by a Minister was deemed to be "limited" in its impact and thus exempted by Art.37. The function in question involved excusing people from the requirement to obtain planning permission. The effects of denying an exemption were not sufficiently serious (the denied person could still get planning permission by the normal process). The Minister *could* thus perform this judicial function, it being limited in its impact.

Example: Similarly in *Melton Enterprises v Censorship of Publications Board* [2004] 1 I.L.R.M. 260 the Supreme Court concluded that while the functions of the Censorship Board may have been judicial in nature, they were limited in scope. Comparing the potential consequences to those in the *Re Solicitors' Act* case noted above, the court concluded that a ban on the distribution of a specific publication was neither as profound nor as far-reaching as losing one's right to a carry on a profession. The Board's powers to censor publications were thus upheld as constitutional.

The court noted, moreover, that while the allegations of indecency and obscenity might also have provided the basis for a separate criminal prosecution this did not mean that the Board was considering criminal matters within the meaning of Art.37. A "criminal matter", according to *State (Murray) v McRann* [1979] I.R. 133, necessarily involves "a procedure associated with the prosecution of a person for a crime". The ultimate question in such matters is whether a crime has been committed. The censorship of a publication did not constitute a decision that anyone had committed a crime; simply that the general moral wellbeing demanded that certain publications should not be publicly available.

In summary one must ask:

(a) Is the function a judicial function?
- If not—it *can* be performed by a body other than a court.
- If so—proceed to (b).
(b) If it is a judicial function, does it deal with a criminal matter?
- If so—it can *only* be performed by a court.
- If not—proceed to (c).
(c) Is this judicial function limited in its effects?
- If so—it *can* be performed by a body other than a court.
- If not—it can *only* be performed by a court.

14. THE RIGHTS OF A SUSPECT: ARREST, DETENTION AND TRIAL

As a general principle, a person has the right to liberty. A person cannot be detained by the State unless certain formal procedures have been followed. Indeed, even where a person has been lawfully detained or imprisoned, that person continues to enjoy certain rights, the infringement of which may render the detention illegal.

Rights on arrest

A person generally may only be arrested for the sole purpose of that person being charged with a crime. Such a charge must be laid in the presence of a judge, typically a judge of the District Court. Where a person has been arrested that person enjoys certain rights:

- the right to be informed of the charges against him or her (*People (DPP) v Walsh* [1980] I.R. 294);
- the right to be charged before the District Court at the earliest possible opportunity;
- the right to have access to and to consult with a lawyer (*People (DPP) v Healy* [1990] I.L.R.M. 313);
- the right to free legal aid, if required (*State (Healy) v Donoghue* [1976] I.R. 325);
- the right to medical treatment, if required;
- the right to remain silent (subject to certain exceptions) and the right to be told of that right;
- the right to be given food and time to sleep; and
- the right not to be oppressively interrogated.

The infringement of any of these rights may lead to the arrest being deemed illegal.

Detention for questioning—general rule

It is generally understood that an arrest cannot be made for the purposes of questioning a suspect. At common law, the sole purpose of an arrest is said to be that of bringing the accused before a court of law for the purpose of charging that person with an offence. While a person may voluntarily respond to questions posed by the Gardaí, it is generally his or her right to remain silent in the face of such questioning. As a general rule, moreover, a person cannot be penalised for remaining silent during such questioning.

Detention for questioning—special provisions

Generally an arrested person must be charged before a court of law at the earliest possible opportunity. In some cases, however, Acts of Parliament qualify the common law position by allowing a person to be arrested and detained for questioning:

- **Section 30 of the Offences Against the State Act 1939.** A person arrested in respect of certain "scheduled" offences designated by that Act may be detained for the purpose of investigating that offence. Such detention may continue for up to 24 hours, renewable at the end of that period for another 24 hours. Since 1998, moreover, a District Court judge may extend the period of detention by a further 24 hours, bringing the total period of possible detention to three days.

- **Section 4 of the Criminal Justice Act 1984 (as amended by the Criminal Justice Act 2006).** A person arrested in respect of any offence attracting five or more years' imprisonment may be detained for questioning for up to six hours. This period may be extended to a maximum total of 24 hours. (A similar provision can be found in s.42 of the Criminal Justice Act 1999, allowing a maximum detention period of 24 hours in respect of certain alleged offences.)

- **Criminal Justice (Drug Trafficking) Act 1996.** Persons arrested on suspicion of drug trafficking may be detained for questioning, initially for up to six hours. Such period of detention, however, may be extended by a further 18 hours and then by another 24 hours, in both cases with the consent of a Chief Superintendent Garda. A District Court judge, where requested to do so, may extend this period of detention by a further 72 hours and then again by 48 hours. (The total possible period amounts to seven days.) (See also s.50, Criminal Justice Act 2007 which, likewise, allows a person charged with serious offences involving firearms and explosives to be detained on arrest for up to seven days.)

The constitutionality of detention for questioning

Ordinarily, arrest and detention cannot be used for the purpose of questioning. Nonetheless, the Supreme Court has ruled that special provisions allowing detention for questioning in appropriately serious cases are not unconstitutional provided they are proportionate and justified by the public interest in combating serious crime (see *People (DPP) v Quilligan (No. 1)* [1987] I.L.R.M. 606). Additionally, certain constitutional safeguards arise in respect of such questioning:

- **Garda questioning cannot be oppressive.** The courts have stipulated that where a person is being detained for questioning, he or she continues to enjoy certain constitutional rights, such as the right to a lawyer and to medical treatment, if needed. In particular, the Constitution requires that any questioning that is conducted is not oppressive. It would, for instance, be unconstitutional to "exhaust" a confession out of an accused through lengthy questioning with no break. In *People (DPP) v McNally* (1981) 2 Frewen 43, a confession that followed 40 continuous hours of questioning was deemed to have been inadmissible in the accused's trial, such that the accused's conviction (and that of a co-accused) was quashed. Likewise, in *People (DPP) v Lynch* [1982] I.R. 64, a statement made after 22 hours' questioning without sleep was excluded on the grounds of oppression.

- **Confessions must be voluntary.** A confession that is the product of pressures, threats or inducements, physical or psychological, will not be admissible in an accused's trial. Nor will confessions made while the accused is under the influence of alcohol, hypnosis or a controlled drug (see Griffin J. in *People (DPP) v Shaw* [1982] I.R. 1).

The right to bail

It is always the case that a person, until found guilty by a court of law, is assumed innocent of all wrongdoing. This means that where a person has been charged with an offence, he is assumed to be innocent of that offence until proven guilty. As a corollary to this right, it was formerly the case that a person who had been arrested or charged with an offence was entitled to be released on bail pending trial. When bail is granted, a suspect may be released on the condition that he or she returns to court to face trial. To ensure that this happens, the suspect may be asked to deposit a sum of money that will be forfeited if the suspect does not turn up for trial.

Prior to 1997, bail could only be denied in two specific cases, namely where the court had a well-founded fear either:

•   that it was likely that the suspect would "skip bail" and not face trial; or
•   that the suspect would use his time on bail to intimidate witnesses to the alleged crime or otherwise interfere with evidence.

It was not possible, in particular, to refuse bail on the grounds that the court believed that the accused would "reoffend" while on bail (see *People (Attorney General) v O'Callaghan* [1966] I.R. 501 and *Ryan v DPP* [1989] I.R. 399). To assume this would, the courts believed, presuppose that the suspect was guilty of the crimes of which he was accused, an assumption that infringed the right to be presumed innocent until proven guilty.

In 1996, however, the Constitution was amended to restrict the circumstances in which bail might be granted. Under the terms of the Sixteenth Amendment to the Constitution (Art.40.4.6°), it is now possible to deny bail to a suspect "where it is reasonably considered necessary to prevent the commission of a serious offence by that person". On foot of this amendment, the Bail Act 1997 was enacted. Under the Act, bail may be denied where the suspect is accused of specified "serious offences" as listed in the Schedule to the Act (they include murder, rape and certain offences involving firearms and/or explosives). A serious offence is further defined as an offence attracting a maximum penalty not less than five years' imprisonment.

In deciding whether to deny bail, the court must have regard to the following:

•   the degree of seriousness of the offence;
•   the strength of the evidence against the accused;
•   the likely sentence that the accused may be given, if convicted;
•   any previous convictions that the accused has attracted (especially for crimes committed while on bail);
•   the fact that the accused has a drug addiction; and
•   the likelihood that the accused will commit a crime while on bail.

Further restrictions on bail were imposed under the Criminal Justice Act 2007, including the right to tag some persons on bail with electronic monitors (see s.11).

The right to silence

Generally, a person who is arrested on suspicion of a crime cannot be forced to answer questions put to him. This is called the right to silence, or the "privilege against self-incrimination". (In the United States a similar right arises from the Fifth Amendment to the US Constitution, which gives rise to the phrase "pleading the Fifth", meaning to claim one's right to silence.) An important aspect of this right is that a court cannot ordinarily draw any inferences or conclusions from a person's silence. One cannot assume, thus, that a person's silence in the face of accusation implies guilt.

In *Heaney v Ireland* [1994] 3 I.R. 593, the Supreme Court ruled that the right to silence is a constitutional right protected by Art.40.6 of the Constitution as a corollary to the right of free expression. The right to silence, however, is not absolute. It has to be balanced against the public's right to be protected against crime. Thus, in *Heaney* itself, the Supreme Court ruled that an Act of Parliament was constitutional even though it made it an offence to refuse, when arrested, to answer questions concerning the suspect's whereabouts at a particular time. In this case, the court concluded that the Act struck an appropriate and proportionate balance between respecting the rights of the prisoner and protecting the public generally. (Though in *Heaney v Ireland* (2001) 33 E.H.R.R. 264, the European Court of Human Rights determined that the same measure infringed Art.6 of the E.C.H.R.).

Example: Sections 18 and 19 of the Criminal Justice Act 1984 (as amended by the Criminal Justice Act 2007) allow the Gardaí to question persons who have been arrested under this legislation. Such a person may be questioned in relation to any object, substance or mark that is found in his possession, on his person, on his clothing or footwear or in the place where he has been arrested. The person may also be asked to account for their presence in that place. This includes situations where people are arrested in possession of what appears to be an illegal drug or stolen property, or where the person has a needle mark on his body. Failure to answer questions posed by the police concerning these matters may lead to the court drawing conclusions from such silence regarding a person's guilt. (At the time of questioning, the accused must be informed of these possible consequences). Such conclusions (or "inferences"), however, may only be drawn if supported by "corroborating" evidence that endorses such conclusions.

In *Rock v Ireland* [1997] 3 I.R. 484, a suspect was arrested in possession of what turned out to be counterfeit US dollars. His failure to answer questions regarding his possession of these items led to certain inferences being drawn under ss.18 and 19 of the Criminal Justice Act. The Supreme Court again concluded, however, that these provisions had not breached the suspect's right to silence. The court considered that the legislation, as in *Heaney,* represented an appropriate balance between the rights of the accused and the interests of the public at large.

In this context it is worth noting also the provisions of s.30 of the Criminal Justice Act 2007. This allows inferences to be drawn where a person, who is arrested for certain serious offences fails, prior to or at the time of being charged, to raise a point that is later used in his defence, if the circumstances of arrest clearly demand an explanation from the accused. Hence, the fact that a person did not attempt to demonstrate their innocence at the time of arrest may subsequently be used against them. This appears to demand of an accused, at the time of arrest, a declaration of innocence that may run counter to the right to silence. Nonetheless, on the authority of *Rock* the prospect of this measure being struck down seems slim.

Fairness in the trial of offences

Article 38.1 of the Constitution requires that no person be tried in relation to an alleged offence except "in due course of law". This means that a criminal trial may only proceed in accordance with the law and, in particular, with reference to certain rules of fairness. The trial, in other words, must be a fair trial. The following are some of the main principles of a fair trial.

The crime must be one known to the law

A person cannot be charged with a crime unless that crime is one recognised in law. In particular, it is necessary that the charges against the person relate to a specific activity that is expressly deemed in law to be illegal. It would be unconstitutional, for instance, to prosecute a person for a "breach of the law" if the particular aspect of the relevant law is not specified or made clear to the accused and to the court.

Example: In the *People (Attorney General) v Edge* [1943] I.R. 115, the Supreme Court held that the defendant could not be convicted of "kidnapping" a minor with the minor's consent but against the will of his parents. This was because the alleged offence (in the words of O'Byrne J.) was "not an indictable offence at common law" [1943] I.R. 146. There was, in short, no such offence known to the law at that time.

A criminal offence cannot be created retrospectively

Article 15.5 of the Constitution states that the Oireachtas cannot make something a crime with retrospective effect, that is, to render something a crime that was not a crime at the time of its commission. Thus, if the Government were to ban gambling on Friday, it would not be permissible to backdate the new law to cover a bet that was legally made the previous Tuesday.

The presumption of innocence

A person accused of a crime is entitled to be considered innocent of the crime until proven guilty. In *O'Leary v Attorney General* [1993] 1 I.R. 102 and *Hardy v Ireland* [1994] 2 I.R. 550 alike, the Supreme Court acknowledged that this common law right was also a right protected by Art.38.1 of the Constitution. This means, for instance, that a person who has previously been convicted of stealing 100 cars on 100 separate occasions is still entitled to the presumption that he is innocent when accused of stealing another car. From this right springs the rule that a suspect may only be convicted where there is no reasonable doubt as to his guilt. There is moreover, no requirement on the accused to prove his innocence. In other words, the onus or burden of proving his guilt beyond a reasonable doubt is on the prosecution.

Example: In *King v Attorney General* [1981] I.R. 233, the Supreme Court ruled that a provision making it a crime for a "suspected person or reputed thief" to "loiter with intent" was unconstitutional. Integral to the offence was the condition of being a "suspected" or "reputed" wrongdoer. This essentially presupposed that a person with a bad reputation was guilty of a crime, this being a breach of the presumption of innocence.

The flip side of the presumption of innocence is that the accused generally cannot be obliged to prove his innocence. Sometimes, however, the "evidential burden" of disproving particular matters is cast onto the accused. This places on the accused the onus of having to disprove, for instance, certain inferences that might otherwise be drawn from evidence.

Example: In *O'Leary v Attorney General* [1993] 1 I.R. 102, the accused had been convicted of membership of an illegal organisation. When arrested, Mr O'Leary had been found in possession of 37 posters depicting a man brandishing a rifle and the words "IRA call the shots". The law under which he was convicted stated that the possession of such "incriminating documents" would constitute "evidence until the contrary is proved" that the person belonged to an illegal organisation. The Supreme Court rejected a claim that this measure infringed the presumption of innocence. It observed that throughout the plaintiff's trial, the overall onus of proving membership of an illegal organisation was on the prosecution. The provision in question simply provided evidence (and not proof) of such membership. While this evidence may have made it substantially easier to convict the accused, it did not shift the overall burden of proving the guilt of the accused.

Example: Similar provisions were also unsuccessfully challenged in *Hardy v Ireland* [1994] 2 I.R. 550. The legislation in question in that case stated that a person found in possession of an explosive substance would be guilty of an offence, unless that person could show that the explosives were to be used for a lawful purpose. This "reverse-onus" provision was again upheld. The Supreme Court noted that it simply moved the evidential burden (and not the overall burden of proof) onto the accused. It rendered such possession evidence but not proof of the accused's guilt, evidence that could be contradicted by evidence of a lawful purpose.

In this context, one might note the terms of s.15C of the Misuse of Drugs Act 1977 (enacted by the Criminal Justice Act 2006). This section raises a presumption that unless it is established to the contrary, a person found in possession of drugs in the vicinity of a prison or remand centre, in circumstances that indicate that they are not for that person's own use, intends illegally to convey the drugs into the prison. On the authority of *Hardy* and *O'Leary* such a provision would more than likely be upheld.

The right to a speedy trial

Although the wheels of law typically move at a slow pace, an accused cannot be denied the right to clear his name indefinitely. Thus, where there has been a prejudicial delay in the commencement of a trial, the trial may not be allowed to proceed. Although there is no statute of limitations on criminal prosecutions, it is clear that an unreasonable and excessive delay in proceeding to trial may prevent prosecution where the delay would likely result in prejudice to the accused.

Example: In *State (O'Connell) v Fawsitt* [1986] I.L.R.M. 639, the accused, who had first been charged in 1981, was not tried until 1985. There having been no good reason for this inordinate delay, the Supreme Court ruled that the trial could not proceed. Of particular note was the fact that by the time the case came up for trial, an important defence witness was no longer available to testify. In these circumstances, the court concluded, the accused could not be guaranteed a fair trial.

Example: In *N.C. v DPP* [1991] 1 I.R. 471, a nine-year delay in raising a complaint of sexual abuse was deemed to have diminished the accused's right to a fair trial. A key point in the case was the unexplained nature of the delay: no good reason could be given for the delay. There was evidence, moreover, that the delay might have prejudiced the accused's right to a fair trial.

That said, much longer periods of delay may result in a successful prosecution. There is no fixed period of time after which a criminal trial cannot proceed. Indeed, several cases have been successfully prosecuted many decades after the alleged offence was committed. The question that arises here is whether the delay has been so extensive to the point of being "excessive and prejudicial", undermining the right to a fair trial (See *H. v DPP* [2006] I.E.S.C. 55). This is a matter to be considered in each individual case by reference to the facts of that case. Here, one has to balance the legitimate interest in vindicating victims' rights with the accused's right to a fair trial. The length of time between the alleged offence and the prosecution thereof may affect the accused's ability to defend himself. Witnesses may, in the meantime, have forgotten crucial facts, or may, indeed, have died. On the other hand, if the court believes that a fair trial is still possible, the case may proceed. A delay may arise for very legitimate reasons: due for instance, to the psychological state of a witness, or where scientific evidence of guilt not available at the time the offence was committed subsequently comes to light due to innovations in forensic science.

Particular problems arise in the context of accusations of sexual assault upon children, some of which are first reported as many as 30 or 40 years after the crimes in question were allegedly committed. In

B. v DPP [1997] 2 I.L.R.M. 118, for instance, a man had been accused of having sexually abused his three daughters over a period of time that ended some 20–30 years before the case came to trial. This delay was not due to any fault on the part of either the daughters or the State. The trial was allowed to proceed even after this delay, the Supreme Court ruling that there was no real risk that the accused would not obtain a fair trial. That said, Denham J. noted that the trial judge in this case would have to give "appropriate directions" where it was felt that the passage of time may have diminished the reliability of evidence or other matters.

The right to be present at one's trial

A suspect has the right to be present at his trial. In the *People (Attorney General) v Messitt* [1972] I.R. 204, a trial that proceeded after the accused had been forcibly removed from the court for misbehaviour, was deemed to have been unconstitutional, highly prejudicial evidence against the accused having been heard in his absence. Where the accused's absence, however, is voluntary or self-imposed (as, for instance, in *People (Attorney General) v Kelly* [1982] I.L.R.M. 1, where the suspect had absconded during his trial), the accused will generally be considered to have waived this right.

The ability to understand the proceedings

An accused person has the right to an interpreter in cases where he or she does not sufficiently understand the language in which the proceedings are being heard. Similar considerations apply in the case of persons who are deaf or hard of hearing (i.e. such persons would have the right to a sign language interpreter). This right flows from the principle that an accused must be able to understand the proceedings of the trial. For example, in *State (Buchan) v Coyne* (1936) 70 I.L.T.R. 185, a conviction was quashed on the grounds that the accused, a Scotsman, was unable to understand Irish, the language in which the trial had been heard. As he had not been afforded an interpreter, his conviction was deemed unsafe.

The right to an impartial judge and jury

An accused person is entitled to a fair trial in front of a judge (or, where relevant, a jury), who is (or are) impartial and independent. The principle that is said to apply in this context is *nemo iudex in causa sua*, that is, that one cannot be a judge in one's own cause. Thus, where a judge or juror has a vested interest in the result of a case, that person will not be permitted to hear the case. For instance, in *People (Attorney General) v Singer* [1975] I.R. 408, the decision of a jury that convicted the defendant was quashed on the grounds that the foreman was a victim of the *specific* alleged fraud in respect of which the accused was being tried.

A trial may also be suspended where pre-trial publicity, for instance in the media, might threaten the accused's prospects of getting a fair trial before a jury. Thus in *Magee v O'Dea* [1994] 1 I.R. 500, Flood J. refused to allow the extradition of the plaintiff, on the grounds that his right to a fair trial had been prejudiced by unfavourable comments in the UK media.

The right to a certain and proportionate sentence

Any sentence handed down on conviction must be certain (in the sense that it has a definite beginning and end) and proportionate ("the punishment fits the crime"). In *Cox v Ireland* [1992] 2 I.R. 503 a measure preventing a convicted person from working for the State for seven years following a conviction was struck down as disproportionate relative to the seriousness of his crime. The section in question allowed a person to be sacked in respect of offences some of which were in fact relatively minor. *Lovett v Minister for Education* [1997] I.L.R.M. 89, concerned a measure that sought to nullify the pension of a retired teacher on imprisonment for more than 12 months. This, Kelly J. concluded, was disproportionate in that the severe penalty far outstripped the relatively minor nature of some of the crimes to which it was applied. In both cases the courts noted that the offences were not of sufficient seriousness to justify the significant restriction of the plaintiffs' property rights.

In *State (O.) v O'Brien* [1973] I.R. 50, provisions allowing a juvenile convict to be imprisoned until the Minister for Justice saw fit to release him were deemed to be unconstitutional, partly on the ground that the length of the sentence was indeterminate. (See also *State (Keating) v Ó hUadaigh* unreported, High Court, December 4, 1976.)

This point was again considered in *Whelan and Lynch v Minister for Justice, Equality and Law Reform* unreported, High Court, Irvine

J., October 5, 2007, but this time unsuccessfully. There, Irvine J. rejected the proposition that a mandatory life sentence for murder could potentially breach the requirement of proportionality. There was, she concluded "… nothing offensive in the Oireachtas promoting the respect for life by concluding that any murder even at the lowest end of the scale, is so abhorrent and offensive to society that it merits a mandatory life sentence." Nor did this infringe the requirement of proportionality, the Oireachtas being entitled to restrict one's liberty for life as punishment even "for the lowest order of murderous activity".

The right to silence

See above at pp.111–112.

The rule against double jeopardy

At common law, a person has the right not to be tried for a specific offence of which he has already been properly tried. This is called the rule against "double jeopardy". The constitutional standing of this principle was confirmed in *State (O'Callaghan) v Ó hUadaigh* [1977] I.R. 42. The original trial in this case resulted in most of the charges being struck out by the judge. Finlay P. agreed that it would be unfair subsequently to allow the prosecution to keep trying until they obtained a conviction.

Nonetheless, in the *People (DPP) v O'Shea* [1982] I.R. 384, the Supreme Court ruled that it was possible for the DPP to appeal an acquittal by the High Courts, the principle of double jeopardy notwithstanding. This was because of the explicit right in Art.34.4.3° of the Constitution to appeal any decision of the High Court to the Supreme Court, an acquittal being such a "decision". This exception only applies, however, where a person has been acquitted before the High Court.

It is clear that a person may be retried after an acquittal due to the lack of jurisdiction of a court, the person not having been in "jeopardy" during such trial (i.e. because the court lacked jurisdiction to convict). It appears also that a person may be retried after a conviction has been quashed on appeal (see s.5 of the Courts of Justice Act 1928). If, however, a person has been properly acquitted before a fully competent court, he or she cannot normally be retried in respect of the same offence. Several statutes also guard against the possibility of a person tried in one state being tried in respect of the same offence in another jurisdiction.

The right to prepare and present a defence (with legal representation where desired)

A person has the right to defend himself in court. As a corollary, an accused party has the right to adequate time, facilities and expertise to prepare an adequate defence. An accused generally has the right, also, to confront his or her accusers and in particular to cross-examine witnesses for the prosecution so that the accuracy of their evidence may be tested.

This right can, however, be qualified with a view to protecting the right of the victims of alleged crimes. In *Donnelly v Ireland* [1998] 1 I.R. 325, an accused person challenged the provisions of the Criminal Evidence Act 1992. The Act allows the evidence of a child alleged to have been a victim of sexual abuse to be given in a separate room and broadcast into open court via a live video link. This, Mr Donnelly alleged, denied him the right to confront his accuser. The Supreme Court, however, ruled that the Act did not breach the accused's rights. The Act still permitted the cross-examination of the alleged victim, during which time the jury could observe the reactions and demeanour of the witness. The Act was, the court suggested, a fair balance of the rights of the accused with those of the alleged victim, who might be unduly traumatised by an appearance in open court.

As another aspect of the right to defend oneself, an accused person has the right to a lawyer, both following arrest and during trial. This is an essential safeguard of the accused's rights, designed to ensure that the accused has access to a skilled advocate who will assist him in his defence. Where a person cannot afford a lawyer, according to *State (Healy) v Donoghue* [1976] I.R. 325, the State is obliged to grant legal aid for the provision of such a lawyer. This is not to say, however, that an accused cannot be tried where he refuses (for reasons other than lack of funds) the assistance of a lawyer. An accused is perfectly entitled to choose to mount his own defence, unassisted by legal representatives.

The position of unconstitutionally obtained evidence

It is generally not possible for a court to use evidence that has been obtained in breach of the Constitution. For instance, it is usually necessary to obtain an accurate search warrant before conducting a search of a person's home. To conduct such a search without a warrant would be in breach of Art.40.5 guaranteeing the "inviolability of the dwelling place" of the citizen. Any evidence collected during such an unconstitutional search, furthermore, could not be "admitted" (used in evidence) in a court of law.

To this rule there are two broad exceptions.

- **The breach is accidental.** In *People (Attorney General) v O'Brien* ([1965] I.R. 142), a search warrant had been issued intending to permit the search of a specific home (House A). The warrant, however, incorrectly specified the wrong address (House B). When the police searched House A, they discovered certain items that they sought to have entered into evidence in a criminal trial. Yet because of the error the search was technically unconstitutional. Nevertheless, the Supreme Court ruled that the evidence could be admitted, this being a merely accidental and not a deliberate breach of rights. **N.B.** One should not mistake an ignorant but intentional breach of rights for an accidental breach. It is no defence for a Garda who has intentionally collected evidence in breach of the Constitution to say that he did not realise it was unconstitutional to do so.

- **There are "extraordinary excusing circumstances" justifying the breach.** A court may consider unconstitutionally obtained evidence where the circumstances surrounding its collection justify excusing the breach of the Constitution. For example, in *People (DPP) v Shaw* [1982] I.R. 1, the Supreme Court allowed the introduction of evidence that had been collected while the defendant was being unlawfully detained (contrary to his right to liberty (Art.40.4)). In this case the Gardaí had detained the suspect after arrest in excess of the period permitted by law. The Gardaí did this, however, with a view to preventing the likely death of a woman whom the suspect had allegedly kidnapped. The right to life of the kidnapped woman taking precedence over the right to liberty, the court concluded that there were extraordinary circumstances excusing the breach of the defendant's rights.

Similarly, in the *People (DPP) v Lawless* (1985) 3 Frewen 30, an otherwise unlawful Garda search of a house was justified on the grounds that the search was necessary to prevent the imminent destruction of evidence. At the time of the search, the defendant had been attempting to dispose of a quantity of heroin. Again, this amounted to an extraordinary excusing circumstance that permitted the evidence acquired during this search to be admitted.

Criminal intent and the Constitution

While ignorance of the law is no defence, the law generally requires that a person should not be convicted of a crime if he lacks mens rea, that is, if he is not aware that he is carrying out the criminal act (whether or not he knows it is an offence.) Subject to some exceptions, the Constitution generally prohibits the criminalisation of persons who are mentally innocent of wrongdoing.

In *Re Article 26 and the Employment Equality Bill 1996* [1997] 2 I.R. 321, the Supreme Court ruled that an attempt to criminalise a person in respect of an act of which they had no knowledge infringed Arts 38.1 and 40.1 of the Constitution. A provision of the Bill stipulated that an employer could be held vicariously liable for the actions of its employees, even if the employer itself had no knowledge of those actions, and had not approved such actions. The penalty for breach was a maximum fine of £15,000 (€19,050) and/or a term of imprisonment of up to two years. This, the court reasoned, constituted a breach of Art.38.1 of the Constitution in that it purported to impose very severe criminal sanctions "… in circumstances which are so unjust, irrational and inappropriate would make any purported trial of such a person not one held in due course of law."

Similarly, in *C.C. v Ireland* [2006] I.E.S.C. 33, the Supreme Court struck down a law criminalising sexual intercourse with a person under the age of 15, on the basis that the relevant measure potentially penalized the mentally innocent. The plaintiff in this case had been charged with unlawful carnal knowledge of a girl under the age of 15, though he had been led to believe, at the time, that she was 16. The Act, however, did not excuse a mistake as to age. This effectively meant that the accused could be convicted despite the fact that he was not aware that the girl was under 15. The section, Hardiman J. concluded, "… contains no balance: it wholly removes the mental element and expressly criminalises the mentally innocent." As a result, the court ruled that the measure infringed Art.40.3 of the Constitution, in that it unfairly denied the plaintiff his right to liberty and to his good name under that Article. The court noted in particular the heavy penalty for the crime in question (life imprisonment), and the significant social stigma attaching to a conviction under the Act.

A key element of this decision is that where a person is accused of a crime, the situation and in particular the state of mind of the individual is key to the consideration of guilt or innocence. In *C.C.*, Hardiman J. rejected the proposition that the general protection of young girls justified denying a defence of mistake as to age.

Trial by jury

Every person who is tried on foot of a criminal charge must be tried before a jury, *except* in three specified cases:

- where the offence is a "minor" offence;
- where the offender is being tried before the Special Criminal Court; or
- where the offender is being tried before a court martial (i.e. in accordance with military law).

What is a "minor" offence?

A "minor" offence is an offence that may be tried without a jury, before what is called a court of "summary" jurisdiction (with a judge and no jury). While the Constitution does not expressly define what is "minor" for these purposes, the courts have ruled that in determining this matter *one must look primarily to the severity of the maximum penalty that might be imposed if a person is found guilty of an offence.*

In *Melling v Ó Mathghamnhna* [1962] I.R. 1, the Supreme Court observed that while one must look to the moral quality of the act and the state of the law and public opinion at the time that the Constitution was enacted, the primary consideration in determining whether an offence is or is not minor is the *severity of the maximum penalty available for that offence.*

As a rough guide it is suggested that, currently an offence attracting a maximum penalty of *more than one year in prison* and/or a *fine of €3,000* or more would constitute a non-minor offence.

One might consider briefly some cases in which the courts had to consider whether an offence was minor or not:

- In *Conroy v Attorney General* [1965] I.R. 411, the Supreme Court ruled that a driving offence attracting a maximum penalty of six months in prison was a minor offence.
- By contrast, according to *Mallon v Minister of Agriculture* [1996] 1 I.R. 517, an offence attracting a possible penalty of two years in prison would not be a minor offence.
- In *Kostan v Ireland* [1978] I.L.R.M. 12, a fishing offence that resulted in the confiscation of a boat worth €128,570 was deemed to be a non-minor offence, owing to the size of the penalty.
- In *O'Sullivan v Hartnett* [1983] I.L.R.M. 79, it was suggested that a fine of €2,300 would have made the relevant offence a "non-minor" offence.

Primary v secondary punishment

In taking into account the severity of an offence the court may only look to the sentence that might be handed down and *not to any other secondary consequences* that flow from being found guilty. In determining whether an offence is non-minor, the court is thus not entitled to have regard to any consequential side-effects of a finding of guilt not formally imposed as part of the sentence, such as the consequent loss of employment or the loss of a statutory licence. For instance, in *State (Pheasantry) v Donnelly* [1982] I.L.R.M. 512, a publican had been found guilty of several successive licensing offences. He asserted that because he stood to lose his licence to sell alcohol as a result of these offences, the third such offence should not have been treated as a minor offence. The High Court refused to accept this argument: in considering the severity of a penalty the court need only look to the primary punishment and not to any secondary consequential injury that the convict would suffer as a side-effect of the verdict. (See also *Charlton v Ireland* [1984] I.L.R.M. 39, where the loss of a bookmaker's licence subsequent to conviction was deemed to be secondary only, and not relevant to the issue of whether the offence was non-minor.)

Example: In *Conroy v Attorney General* [1965] I.R. 411, the Supreme Court held that a drink–driving offence, the maximum penalty for which was six months' imprisonment, was a minor offence. This was despite the fact that the law also required that a person found guilty of such an offence would lose his licence to drive for one year thereafter. Even though quite severe consequences might flow from the loss of the licence, the court found that this was a "secondary consequence" that could not on its own lift the offence into the category of non-minor offences.

It might be argued that the distinction is not particularly convincing. The court must be aware that the loss of a licence of the type considered above can have a very significant effect on the livelihood of the individual. Although the punishment may not be imposed directly by the court, the consequence flows inevitably from the conviction, such that it is at least arguable that these very real and significant consequences should be considered.

The Special Criminal Court

Article 38.3 allows for the establishment of Special Courts for the trial of offences. The key feature of these courts is that instead of a jury, the accused is tried before three judges drawn from the ordinary courts of the State. This means that an accused is effectively deprived, in such cases, of his right to a trial by jury.

In a nutshell, these courts are established where the State fears that a jury would be intimidated or threatened by persons connected to the accused. Thus trials before the Special Criminal Court tend to involve accused persons alleged to be associated with known terrorist organisations and criminal gangs.

Provision is made for the establishment of a Special Criminal Court in the Offences Against the State Act 1939. Part V of that Act allows the Government to set up such a court whenever it considers that "the ordinary courts are inadequate to secure the effective administration of justice and the preservation of public peace and order". The Government's view in this regard is not subject to judicial review, i.e. the establishment and use of the Special Criminal Court cannot be challenged in a court of law (see *Kavanagh v Ireland* [1996] 1 I.R. 321 and *Gilligan v Ireland* [2001] 1 I.L.R.M. 473).

Military courts

Military courts are not subject to the requirement that non-minor criminal offences be tried before a jury. Military law, however, typically applies only to members of the armed forces on active service. In times of peace, members of the public are generally not subject to such courts. These courts are permitted to operate by Art.38.4 and are regulated in the main by the provisions of the Defence Acts 1954–1998.

Trial for contempt of court

Where a person is charged with contempt involving scandalizing the court, prejudicing a fair trial or otherwise interfering with the process of the courts, the right to trial by jury may be limited in order to protect the courts' independence. Effectively, the courts have a right to protect their judicial functions from attack—generally, no jury is required to vindicate this right. In *Murphy v British Broadcasting Corporation* [2004] I.E.H.C. 440 a claim was made that the BBC had allegedly prejudiced the trial of the plaintiff by broadcasting material concerning the Omagh bombing of 1997. The allegation made was that this constituted a contempt of court. McKechnie J. concluded that contempt of court, even where non-minor, did not ordinarily require a trial by jury (though some limited exceptions applied, where the matter was criminal, non-minor and where the facts were in contention). He stressed that the conduct of court cases was a matter exclusively reserved to the judiciary, who were deemed independent in the performance of this function. This independence could not be maintained if the courts "could not master their own destiny". The courts thus were entitled to protect their integrity and dignity against unjust comment, a power that would have been undermined if they had to "... cede any part of [this] self-protecting obligation to a jury".

The general principles of a jury trial

Juries mainly hear non-minor criminal cases. Although the jury has been abolished in most *civil* proceedings, it is still used in defamation cases (libel and slander), and in relation to the torts of false imprisonment and malicious prosecution. Its primary function, however, is to determine the guilt or innocence of accused persons in non-minor trials. In this context, it stands as an important defence against state tyranny, requiring that a person may only be tried before a jury of his peers.

Unless the offence falls within one of the exceptions listed in Arts 38.2–38.4, "no person shall be tried on any criminal charge without a jury". This seems to suggest that even if an accused *preferred no jury*, he would still have to be tried before a jury of his peers (i.e. he would not be able to waive that right). (See *Re Haughey* [1971] I.R. 217 and *Holohan v Donohue* [1986] I.R. 45).

Requirements of a jury trial

A person tried before a jury is entitled to certain safeguards:

- **The jury must be independent and impartial.** In the *People (Attorney General) v Singer* [1975] I.R. 408, a jury verdict was quashed on the grounds that the foreman of the jury had a vested interest in the result. He was in fact a victim of the specific crime that was being tried by that very jury!
- **The jury must be as representative as practicable of society at large.** In *De Burca v Attorney General* [1976] I.R. 38, the Supreme Court struck down as unconstitutional the Juries Act 1927. That Act operated in such a manner as to ensure that the vast majority of juries consisted only of male property owners. While men were automatically selected as jurors, women had to apply to join a jury panel. Furthermore, the law prevented persons who were not the owners of land from serving on juries. Besides infringing the requirement of equality in Art.40.1, the Supreme Court found that this legislation meant that the accused was being deprived of her right to be tried before a "fair cross-section of society".

Jury selection and voting

Today, a panel of jurors is selected at random from the Register of Electors. Specific jurors are then selected from these panels to serve in particular jury trials. Potential jurors must be aged between 18 and 70:

- Certain people are legally precluded from serving on juries. These include persons over 70, Gardaí, qualified lawyers and former judges. Certain people may, moreover, gain exemption from jury service. These include doctors, nurses, pharmacists, persons over 65, religious ministers and full-time students.
- While the Constitution does not set any minimum number of jurors, the Criminal Justice Act 1984 requires that a jury consist of 12 persons. A jury may, however, serve with 11 (but no fewer) members.
- A jury may convict a person by a majority of its members, provided that the verdict has the support of at least 10 members (see also *O'Callaghan v Attorney General* [1993] 2 I.R. 17).

15. EQUALITY

Article 40.1 guarantees that all citizens, as human persons, will be treated as equal before the law. This does not, however, mean that all persons will in all cases be treated alike. The terms of Art.40.1 permit, and in some cases require, that the State have regard to relevant differences, physical, moral and social, between different people. (This is sometimes called the "proviso" to Art.40.1) For instance, it would not be unconstitutional for the State to provide special facilities for physically disabled persons that it does not also afford to persons without disabilities. By the same token, the State is probably entitled to make maternity leave for women more extensive than parental leave for men, the physical burden of pregnancy being obviously more demanding on women than on men. In short, like situations are to be treated in like manner, but relevant differences can be taken into account in formulating the laws and policies of the State.

An example of such different treatment being upheld by reference to the proviso occurred in *Dillane v Ireland* [1980] I.L.R.M. 167. Dillane concerned a prosecution taken by a Garda. The law at that time prevented an accused person (found not guilty at trial) recouping his costs from a Garda who took a prosecution against him. If a private person other than a Garda had taken the prosecution, that person would not have been so exempted and the accused would have been able to recoup his costs. The Supreme Court reasoned that the special treatment of Gardaí in this instance was justified under Art.40.1 as Gardaí held a different social function from that of lay litigants. In short, a Garda in taking such a prosecution was doing so in pursuance of his civic duty and as a service to the public as a whole. This perspective put him or her in a wholly different position to that of a lay prosecutor. As such, the special treatment of Gardaí was justified by the different social function performed by them.

The guarantee of equality has generally proven quite weak. At its most robust it has been used to strike down inequality on grounds of gender and in relation to elections and referenda. In other contexts, however, it has proven too susceptible to justification on grounds that different treatment serves other constitutional interests, or on speculative hypothetical rationales that do not always bear up to scrutiny. That said, the courts have held that the State is entitled generally to uphold the value of equality, even where this might impact on other constitutional rights. In *Portmarnock Golf Club v Ireland* [2005] I.E.H.C. 235, O'Higgins J. in the High Court upheld (obiter) the validity of the Equal Status Act 2000, which potentially prevented clubs from discriminating on various grounds, including gender. In doing so, O'Higgins J. observed that the State had a legitimate interest in promoting the values of equality and non-discrimination across all strands of society.

Instances where unequal treatment has been established

Gender equality

It is generally unconstitutional to treat one gender more favourably than (or indeed just differently from) the other, as several decided cases bear out. For instance, in *De Burca v Attorney General* [1976] I.R. 38, the Supreme Court declared unconstitutional the Juries Act 1927 partly on the grounds that it breached the guarantee of equality. This was because the Act required only men, and not women, to serve on juries. Women could serve on juries, but only if they expressly applied to be made a juror. Men, on the other hand, did not enjoy this general exemption. As a result, before 1976 most juries almost invariably consisted solely of men. (An added ground of unconstitutionality in this case was the fact that the Juries Act 1927 required that all jurors be "property owners".) (See generally above at p.126).

Similarly discriminatory provisions were struck down in *T.O'G. v Attorney General* [1985] I.L.R.M. 61. In that case, a child had been placed for adoption with a married couple. Sadly, before the adoption was finalised the plaintiff's wife died. In these circumstances the law said that a widower (a bereaved husband) could not adopt a child placed with him unless he already had other children in his care. Similar restrictions did not, however, apply to widows. The High Court concluded that the difference in treatment, based on gender, was unconstitutional.

In *McKinley v Minister for Defence* [1992] 2 I.R. 333, the Supreme Court went so far as to *extend* a common law right to women so as to cure an incident of inequality. That case concerned the tort of loss of *consortium,* which involves the loss of a spouse's ability to engage in sexual intercourse because of an injury. The law formerly allowed a husband, but not a wife, to claim damages from the person who caused this injury. In *McKinley,* however, the Supreme Court agreed to extend the common law right to a wife whose husband had been injured with the resultant loss of sexual ability, on the ground that the tort would otherwise be in breach of the guarantee of equality.

A recent example in this context concerns the application of criminal laws that incurred a more serious penalty for sexual assault on a male than for sexual assault on a female. In *S.M. v Ireland* [2007] I.E.H.C. 280, Laffoy J. declared that s.62 of the Offences Against the Person Act 1861 was unconstitutional and had thus not survived the passage of the Constitution. The measure in question imposed a maximum ten-year sentence in respect of sexual assault on a male. The corresponding legislation applicable at the relevant time to sexual assault on a female imposed a much lesser maximum sentence of two years' imprisonment. (The law has since been changed to equalize upwards the maximum penalties, but such reforms operate prospectively only, (i.e. from the date of the reform) and did not apply at the time of the alleged offences (1966–1976)). Thus, at the relevant time, different maximum sentences applied depending on whether the offence was committed against a male or a female. Ruling that there was no rational basis for such differentiation, Laffoy J. struck down s.62 as an unconstitutional breach of the right to equal treatment. There was no legitimate legislative purpose, she concluded, in protecting men more vigorously than women.

Equality in the political process

Given the importance of maintaining the integrity of the democratic process, equality is very much at a premium in the context of elections and referenda. The courts have thus frequently intervened to combat examples of unequal treatment favouring one candidate or side of a referendum or election campaign over another.

Example: In *McKenna v An Taoiseach (No. 2)* [1995] 2 I.R. 10, the Supreme Court ruled that the State's application of funding to promote a "Yes" vote in the divorce referendum of 1995 infringed the constitutional guarantee of equality. The court suggested that extending funds to one side of the campaign, but not the other, breached the equality rights of the citizen by "putting the voting rights of one class of citizen (those in favour of the change) above those of another class of citizen (those against)".

Example: In *Kelly v Minister for the Environment* [2002] 4 I.R. 191 the plaintiff, an aspiring election candidate, challenged the validity of a cap on election spending imposed on all candidates.

While the court agreed that such a cap on spending would normally be legitimate, it noted that the rules exempted from consideration the value of Oireachtas facilities such as free postage, telephone calls and equipment available to existing Members of Parliament who were defending their seats. This, the court concluded, favoured sitting Members over aspiring candidates, an outcome that breached the constitutional guarantee of equality.

Example: Similarly, an imbalance in the time given by public broadcasters to one side of a referendum debate over another is an unconstitutional breach of the guarantee of equality (see *Coughlan v Broadcasting Complaints Commission* [2000] 3 I.R. 1). Similar principles would apply to the coverage of election campaigns.

Other examples

Example: In *McMahon v Leahy* [1984] I.R. 525, the Supreme Court ruled that a prisoner who had escaped from a prison in Northern Ireland in 1975 was entitled to be treated in the same manner as the four other prisoners with whom he had escaped. These four other prisoners had been caught in the Republic sometime previously but had not been extradited back to Northern Ireland because their offences were considered (at that time) to be "political offences". In the intervening period, however, the political offence doctrine had changed such that the accused was no longer able to avail of it. Nonetheless, the Supreme Court ruled that as the accused could not be treated any differently from similarly placed persons, it could not allow his extradition.

Example: In *An Blascaod Mór Teo. v Commissioners of Public Works* [2000] 1 I.L.R.M. 401, the Supreme Court struck down legislation that discriminated between relatives of those born on the Blasket Islands and persons who were not so related. The legislation in question purported to exempt from a compulsory purchase order in respect of the islands any person who was related to a former resident of the islands. This, the court found, breached the requirement that persons be treated equally before the law.

Instances where unequal treatment has not been established

Discrimination must be based on human characteristics

The Constitution only recognises discrimination where based on the human characteristics of an individual and not where the discrimination relates to non-inherent matters, such as the profession or residence of a person. If, for instance, a female lawyer were to allege that she was discriminated against because of her gender (an inherent characteristic) she could claim a breach of Art.40.1. If, on the other hand, she alleged that she had been treated unequally on account of her profession, i.e. because she was a lawyer, she could not claim a breach of the guarantee of equality, a person's profession not being one of her human characteristics. For example, in *Madigan v Attorney General* [1986] I.L.R.M. 136, the Supreme Court ruled that the plaintiff could not invoke Art.40.1 where he was alleging unequal treatment based on his status as a property owner.

Example: In *Quinn's Supermarket v Attorney General* [1972] I.R. 1, the Supreme Court ruled that a legal person, such as a company, was not entitled to rely on the equality guarantee as Art.40.1 refers only to "human persons". In the course of its decision, the court went on to note that the right to be treated equally: "... refers to human persons for what they are in themselves rather than to any lawful activities, trades or pursuits which they engage in or follow".

Where the inequality may be justified on other grounds

In some cases the courts have found that although legal measures discriminate between similarly placed individuals, there may be a good reason for such a distinction to be made. In such cases the equality guarantee will not have been breached.

Example: In *O'B. v S.* [1984] I.R. 316, the Supreme Court ruled that measures that discriminated between children born inside and outside marriage respectively were justified by the constitutional preference for marriage contained in Art.41.3.1°. Thus a law that excluded a child born outside marriage from claiming from the estate of her father (who died without making a will) was not unconstitutional, despite the fact that she would have succeeded in her claim had she been a child born inside marriage.

Example: In *Norris v Attorney General* [1984] I.R. 36, the plaintiff complained that laws that penalised male but not female homosexual sexual activity were in breach of the guarantee of equality between the sexes. The Supreme Court reasoned (though not entirely convincingly) that homosexual behaviour between males posed a greater "threat" to the social order than like female activity. A similarly unconvincing line of argument succeeded in *Somjee v Minister for Justice* [1981]

I.L.R.M. 324, where Keane J. upheld laws that (at that time) made it easier for a woman to acquire citizenship through marriage than a similarly placed male. The court effectively reasoned that the State was entitled to take the view that men potentially posed a greater threat to the security of the State than women, and should thus be treated with more caution.

Example: Another unconvincing example is the argument accepted in *Murphy v Attorney General* [1982] I.R. 241. In that case the Supreme Court accepted that tax provisions that discriminated against married couples in favour of unmarried couples were offset by corresponding privileges enjoyed exclusively by married couples. The court thus reasoned that there had been no breach of Art.40.1 (although it proceeded to find the legislation unconstitutional on foot of the provisions in Art.41; see below at p.166).

Example: See also *Pine Valley v Minister for the Environment* [1987] I.R. 23, discussed above at pp.96–97.

16. PERSONAL RIGHTS

Enumerated v Unenumerated rights

There are some rights that are explicitly ("expressly") mentioned in the text of the Constitution. These are known as "enumerated" rights. They include the right to liberty (Art.40.4), freedom of expression (Art.40.6.1°) and the general right to choose one's own religion (Art.44). Article 40.3.2 also expressly enumerates (sets out) a number of important personal rights, including the right to life discussed below in Ch.17. The right to one's good name and individual property rights are also expressly protected by Art.40.3.2.

Article 40.3.2 requires the State to protect the personal rights of the individual, four specific rights being expressly noted. The Constitution, however, also protects certain rights that are *not* expressly mentioned in the text of the document. For instance, although the Constitution does not explicitly create a right to privacy, it is nonetheless recognised as a constitutional right. Such rights, not explicitly mentioned in the constitutional text, are known as "unenumerated" rights.

On what basis can one recognise a right that is not mentioned in the Constitution?

In *Ryan v Attorney General* [1965] I.R. 294, Kenny J. had to consider whether there was a constitutional right to bodily integrity. There is, it should be noted, no express mention of such a right in the text of the Constitution. Nevertheless, Kenny J. agreed that citizens did enjoy such a right, and that it was, moreover, protected by the Constitution as an "unenumerated" right. Kenny J. looked at the provisions of Art.40.3, which require that the State defend and vindicate certain rights "in particular ... the life, person good, name and property rights of every citizen". The judge pointed out that by using the phrase "in particular", the Article implied that these express rights were not the only rights that warranted protection. Other rights, he concluded, were within the contemplation of the Article, unenumerated rights that, he said, flowed from the "Christian and Democratic nature of the State".

How does one determine the content of these unenumerated rights?

If these rights are not written into the text of the Constitution, how do judges decide what are and what are not constitutional rights? There is no easy answer to this question. Kenny J. suggested that these rights arise from the "Christian and Democratic nature of the State", a test that was cited in *Kennedy v Ireland* [1987] I.R. 587, for example, to support a general right to privacy. Other judges suggest that these rights are "natural rights" that inhere in the individual by virtue of his or her human personality. These are rights, according to Henchy J. in *McGee v Attorney General* [1974] I.R. 284, that are "fundamental to the standing of the individual ... in the context of the social order envisaged by the Constitution."

In fairness, however, neither test takes one particularly far. Each test is vague and leaves judges with a considerable amount of leeway as to what is and what is not a constitutional right. What for example does the term "Christian" entail? In cases of conflict, whose "brand" of Christianity is to be preferred? After all, in *McGee v Attorney General* [1974] I.R. 284, Walsh J. suggested that the courts could not prefer one religious denomination's interpretation of Christian principles over another's.

Natural rights

Similarly, by what criteria do we assess what are "natural" rights? In *Norris v Attorney General* [1984] I.R. 36, for instance, both the majority and the minority in the Supreme Court used natural-law arguments to support diametrically opposed viewpoints. In that case the majority concluded that the constitutional right to privacy did not prohibit a ban on homosexual sexual activity, homosexuality being, as they saw it, "unnatural". The minority by contrast, considered that the ban infringed the natural rights of male homosexuals, one's sexuality being an innate, and thus necessarily a natural characteristic of each individual. It is hard, in short, to escape the conclusion that such widely framed tests give judges too much leeway to "create" rights where none existed before, or to deny them, in accordance with the judges' own personal perspectives.

That said, the Constitution strongly supports the concept of natural rights. Both Arts 41 and 43, for instance, make express reference to natural rights that are "antecedent [prior to] and superior to" *positive law*, that is, "man-made" law. These rights are said to exist not by virtue of law (in other words, no person or parliament *made* or conferred these rights); they simply exist as a feature and consequence of our humanity. These are rights then that exist independently of law; rights that inhere in us by virtue of a higher universal law superior to the State. These rights, moreover, are not "given" to us (except perhaps by God). They exist in each human regardless of the perspective of humankind or of man-made laws (see further above at pp.12–13).

Implied rights

Perhaps the most concrete of the tests for determining the existence of unlisted rights is that of "implication" from enumerated rights. The presence of certain express rights in the Constitution is said necessarily to imply other *implicit* rights. For instance, one could say that the right to practice one's religion (in Art.44) necessarily implies a corollary right *not* to practice a religion. Similarly, the courts have implied from the constitutional right to associate, that is to form unions and associations, a right not to associate, that is to "dissociate" (see *Educational Company v Fitzpatrick (No. 2)* [1961] I.R. 135, and the text below at p.162). In a like manner, the Directives of Social Policy in Art.45, although non-binding in law, have been used to imply an unenumerated right to earn a livelihood (see *Murtagh Properties v Cleary* [1972] I.R. 330, and the text below at pp.137–139).

Some important examples of enumerated rights

The right to one's good name (Art.40.3.2) and the right to liberty (Art.40.4) were both relied upon in *C.C. v Ireland* [2006] I.E.S.C. 33. In that case, the Supreme Court struck down a law criminalising sexual intercourse with a person under the age of 15, on the basis that the measure potentially penalized the mentally innocent. The plaintiff had been charged with unlawful carnal knowledge of a girl under the age of 15. The girl had told him she was 16, a statement that he had believed. The Act, however, did not excuse a mistake as to age. This effectively meant that the accused could be convicted despite the fact that he was not aware that the girl was under 15. Thus, Hardiman J. concluded, "the Section contains no balance: it wholly removes the mental element and expressly criminalises the mentally innocent." As a result, the court ruled that the measure infringed Art.40 of the Constitution, in that it unfairly denied the plaintiff his right to liberty and to his good name under that Article.

The right to one's good name also featured prominently in *Maguire v Ardagh* [2002] 1 I.R. 385. The Oireachtas had set up a special sub-committee to determine the facts surrounding the unfortunate shooting dead of John Carthy in Abbeylara in April 2000. While the sub-committee's findings would have no direct legal effect, there was nonetheless the possibility that a finding of unlawful killing might be made, which would reflect adversely on certain members of the Gardaí.

The Supreme Court concluded that the Oireachtas did not have the inherent power to set up an investigative committee of this nature. In making its decision, the court placed significant emphasis on the potential damage to the good name of the Gardaí in question. While the sub-committee could not penalize a person, the sub-committee's findings as to culpability were nonetheless capable of damaging the good name of a person, contrary to Art.40.3.

Evidently the right to one's good name is vindicated by the tort of defamation (i.e. libel and slander), which allows a person to sue for untrue statements that damage the reputation and standing of the individual.

Some important examples of unenumerated rights

Since the decision in *Ryan v Attorney General* [1965] I.R. 294, the courts have determined the existence of many unenumerated rights. The list of unenumerated rights is not finite and could potentially include a great variety of rights. Here, however, are some of the more important rights that have been identified to date.

The right to bodily integrity

The first "unenumerated" right to be established in a court of law was the right to bodily integrity. In other words, the State cannot behave in a manner that puts citizens and their health in danger. This right was first established in *Ryan v Attorney General* [1965] I.R. 294, where the courts were asked to consider the legality of the fluoridation of public water supplies by the State. Although the courts concluded that there was no proven danger from such fluoridation, both the High Court and the Supreme Court noted that had a danger been established the State would have been liable for breach of the plaintiff's right to bodily integrity.

In *State (Richardson) v Mountjoy Prison* [1980] I.R. 82, a prisoner successfully argued that the insanitary conditions of Mountjoy

Prison's facilities constituted a breach of her right to bodily integrity. The court ruled that the State had failed "to protect the applicant's health" while she was incarcerated.

In *McGee v Attorney General* [1974] I.R. 284, likewise, the Supreme Court ruled that provisions banning the sale or importation of contraceptives infringed the right to bodily integrity of the plaintiff. The plaintiff, who already had four children, ran a serious risk of illness and death if she were to have more children. The provision of contraception having been necessary to prevent such an occurrence, the court ruled that the legislation in question infringed the Constitution by placing the plaintiff at such a risk.

One aspect of the right to bodily integrity relates to the entitlement of a person to refuse medical treatment, even where this will inevitably lead to the death of that person. In *Re a Ward of Court (Withdrawal of Medical Treatment)* [1996] 2 I.R. 79, the Supreme Court ruled that the right to bodily integrity presupposes that a person cannot be made to undergo medical treatment, without that person's consent (see further below at p.145). In exceptional cases, however, it may be possible, with the common good in mind, to force a person to undergo such treatment. This may be possible, for instance, where a person is suffering from a contagious disease that poses a sufficient danger, if left untreated, to the public at large. Here, as elsewhere, the collective interest will be allowed to prevail over that of the individual.

Foley v Sunday Newspapers Ltd [2005] 1 I.R. 89, suggests that a court may be required to curtail the coverage of a trial in the media, where a credible threat to bodily integrity can be established arising from such coverage. While there was insufficient evidence of such a threat in that case, Kelly J. acknowledged that if a convincing case could be made that publicity would endanger the life or bodily integrity of the accused, press coverage could be curtailed.

The right to earn a livelihood

It is unconstitutional for the State, without good reason, to prevent a person from carrying out a legitimate trade or profession for which that person is qualified. This does not, of course, mean that the State is obliged to give everyone a job, still less to guarantee all citizens that they may work in whatever field they so desire.

The first case to establish this right to earn a livelihood was *Murtagh Properties v Cleary* [1972] I.R. 330. This case involved a trade union picket protesting the employment of non-union female bar staff in the plaintiff's public house. Kenny J. held that such actions breached the constitutional right of both the plaintiff and the female staff to earn a livelihood. Kenny J. determined the existence of this right by reference to the (non-binding) Directive Principles of Social Policy, outlined in Art.45 of the Constitution. One of these principles was that "men and women equally" should be entitled to an adequate means of livelihood. This implied, he said, a right to earn a livelihood, protected under Art.40.3.1° as an unenumerated personal right. The union thus could not legally picket the pub. To condone such activity, Kenny J. concluded, would be in breach of the women's right to make their living free from unjust restrictions.

Of course, where the State can show a good reason to prevent a person from working in a particular profession, no right will have been breached. In *Landers v Attorney General* (1973) 109 I.L.T.R. 1, the High Court ruled that a law preventing a young boy from singing in pubs for money was not unconstitutional, the rationale being that such an environment was not a suitable place in which a child should be employed. Employing similar reasoning, it is likely that laws protecting children from exploitation in the labour market to the detriment of their schooling (such as the Protection of Young Persons in Employment Act 1996) would also be constitutional.

It is not, moreover, unconstitutional to prevent a person from working in his chosen profession where that person would pose a danger to the public (such as a convicted paedophile working as a professional child carer) or where the person has broken the law in the course of his employment. In *Hand v Dublin Corporation* [1991] 1 I.R. 409, for instance, the Supreme Court upheld legislation preventing a street trader from obtaining a casual trading licence, the reason being that the trader had twice been convicted of trading without such a licence.

In *Kenny v Dental Council* [2004] I.E.H.C. 29, Gilligan J. ruled that the State was entitled to restrict the practice of dentistry to persons who met certain requirements as to training and competency. The plaintiff, who made dentures for a living, unsuccessfully complained that his right to earn a livelihood had been infringed in circumstances where the Dental Council did not permit him to practice as a denturist. Gilligan J. concluded that the limitation on the right to earn a livelihood in this case was clearly justified by the public health implications of allowing unqualified persons to perform dentistry. By the same token the right to earn a livelihood does not confer an automatic entitlement to access property other than one's own for that purpose (see for instance *Casey v Minister for Arts* [2004] 1 I.R. 402.)

In summary, provided the State can offer a legitimate and sufficiently serious reason for such restriction, it is always possible to curtail the right to earn a livelihood. Such penalties or restrictions must, however, be fair and proportionate. In *Cox v Ireland* [1992] 2 I.R. 503 a measure preventing a convicted person from working for the State for seven years following the conviction was struck down as disproportionate relative to the seriousness of his crime. The severe penalty far outstripped the relatively minor nature of some of the crimes to which it was applied. The offence was not of sufficient seriousness to justify the serious restriction of the plaintiff's property rights as well as his right to earn a livelihood. (See also *Lovett v Minister for Education* [1997] I.L.R.M. 89).

The right to privacy

A person has the general right to privacy, especially in relation to his personal and family affairs. The right to privacy first arose in *McGee v Attorney General* [1974] I.R. 284, a case concerning a legislative ban on the sale or importation of contraception. In that case, the Supreme Court ruled, by a majority, that this prohibition infringed the privacy rights of a married couple. The court felt, in particular, that a married couple was entitled to determine the number of children that the couple might have. By banning access to artificial contraceptives, the State was illegally interfering in what was essentially a family decision.

Yet, the right to privacy is not confined to marital couples. In *Kennedy v Ireland* [1987] I.R. 587, Hamilton P. ruled that by tapping the phones of two journalists without good reason, the State had infringed their individual right to privacy. A key element of this decision was that the State had no legitimate security interest in the conversations of these reporters. The tapping was allegedly effected merely for political purposes. This not being a good reason for tapping a phone, the State was ordered to pay damages to the journalists for the breach of their constitutional right to privacy.

The right to privacy, however, is not an absolute right. The State may, where it has good reason to do so, impinge upon the privacy of a citizen, where for instance it is necessary to protect the security of the State. In *Kearney v Minister for Justice* [1986] I.R. 116, for instance, the High Court ruled that letters sent to a prisoner could be read and censored by prison officials, with the security of the prison in mind. Likewise, the Supreme Court in *Norris v Attorney General* [1984] I.R. 36 ruled that the right to privacy could not be used to invalidate a form of state intrusion that could be justified by reference to the common good. In *Norris* a majority of the Supreme Court ruled that laws that penalised male homosexual sexual activity did not infringe the right to privacy, the majority arguing that the defence of public morality necessitated these measures. (A minority, however, contended that the State had not proved that a liberalisation of the law would endanger the common good.)

The boundaries of the right to privacy were further emphasized in *Redmond v Flood* [1999] 3 I.R. 79, *Caldwell v Mahon* [2006] I.E.H.C. 86 and *Desmond v Moriarty* [2004] 1 I.R. 334, all three cases noting that privacy could be curtailed in order to serve the requirements of the common good. In particular, the public interest in identifying alleged corruption in public office justified the investigation by tribunals of what might be asserted to be matters of private concern.

The right to have children

In *McGee v Attorney General* [1974] I.R. 284, as discussed above, the Supreme Court ruled that the State could not interfere in a family's decision to limit by means of contraception the number of children it produces. In a similar vein, of course, the State cannot prevent families from having children if they so desire. In *Murray v Attorney General* [1991] 1 I.L.R.M. 465, for example, the Supreme Court ruled that, ordinarily, married couples have the right to bear children. In that case, however, the plaintiffs were both prisoners, jailed for life for the murder of a Garda. The court ruled that although the plaintiffs would normally have enjoyed such a right, the requirements of prison security meant that their right had to be restricted. The court accepted that providing conjugal facilities for all married prisoners would significantly compromise prison security. This is, then, a good example of rights being curtailed with a view to promoting the "common good", in this case the public interest in secure prisons.

The right to marry

In *Ryan v Attorney General* it was first suggested (though it was not relevant in that case) that Art.40.3 protected the right to marry. This point was confirmed later in *O'Shea v Ireland* unreported, High Court,

Laffoy J., October 17, 2006. There the High Court struck down a law preventing a man from marrying his brother's former wife (the latter having divorced her former husband, the man's brother). The court agreed that their right to marry had been infringed, further concluding that this infringement was not necessary to protect either the institution of marriage or the common good.

Nonetheless, the right to marry, as currently understood, was deemed in *Zappone and Gilligan v Revenue Commissioners* [2006] I.E.H.C. 404 to be confined to opposite-sex couples, the court ruling that a lesbian couple who had married in Canada were not entitled to be treated as married for tax purposes. Dunne J. concluded that the term "marriage" as used in the Constitution meant heterosexual marriage, there being insufficient evidence of a consensus for change in this regard. It is worth noting that while the right to marry is protected under international law, the European Convention on Human Rights refers to the right of "men and women" to marry and may not thus confer a right on same-sex couples.

The right of access to the courts (the right to litigate)

A person cannot be refused access to justice. In *Macauley v Minister for Post and Telegraphs* [1966] I.R. 345, Kenny J. declared unconstitutional a rule that prevented a case being taken against a Government Minister without the Attorney General's prior approval. Similarly, in *Byrne v Ireland* [1972] I.R. 241 the Supreme Court struck down a rule that prevented ordinary citizens from suing the State. In both cases, an argument that was successfully used was that these measures infringed the general right of the citizen to access the courts of law.

In *Blehein v Minister for Health* [2004] I.E.H.C. 374 a provision of the Mental Treatment Act 1945 restricting legal challenges to a decision to incarcerate mentally ill persons was struck down as an infringement of the right to litigate. The legislation required the patient to seek leave from the High Court prior to litigation, which would only be granted where a substantial case could be made to the effect that the decision to incarcerate was made in bad faith or without reasonable care. Declaring the provision to be unconstitutional, Carroll J. ruled that the permitted grounds for challenge set out in the Act were so narrow as to deny the patient the right to litigate.

It is not, however, unconstitutional generally to restrict a person's access to court on the ground that there has been an inordinate delay in the taking of proceedings. The Statutes of Limitations 1957–2000 (as amended), for instance, set out certain periods of limitation for the taking of cases. If an action is not taken within the period of limitation, it may be deemed to be statute barred, meaning that the defendant can require the court to prevent the litigation from proceeding. In *Tuohy v Courtney* [1994] 3 I.R. 1, the Supreme Court ruled that, provided they were not unreasonably short, periods of limitation were not unconstitutional. The right to litigate, the court reasoned, was subject to the defendant's right to certainty and finality in respect of his potential legal liability.

Nonetheless, where a period of limitation is unreasonably short it may be unconstitutional, especially where there is no provision for the extension of the time limit by a judge. In *White v Dublin City Council* [2004] 1 I.R. 545, for instance, the plaintiffs had not been aware that planning permission had been granted until a two-month limitation period for challenging the decision had expired. As there was no provision for the extension of the period of limitation, the Supreme Court concluded that the limitation period unfairly infringed the constitutional right to litigate. (See also *Brady v Donegal County Council* [1989] I.L.R.M. 182). The crucial point in both *White* and *Brady*, however, was absence of any judicial discretion to extend the deadline, a point illustrated in *Re Article 26 and Sections 5 and 10 of the Illegal Immigrants (Trafficking) Bill, 1999* [2000] 2 I.R. 360. There, a two-week limitation period for judicial review was upheld as constitutional, the crucial difference being that the court in this case was afforded the discretion to reopen the period of limitation in cases of particular hardship.

The right to legal representation

It is well established that a person is entitled to legal representation in both criminal and civil cases before the courts, though the right to financial support for legal representation is generally limited to criminal cases. This is a necessary corollary to the right to litigate and to access the courts.

The right to legal representation extends also to situations in which a person is required to give evidence to an inquiry or administrative body, where the good name and reputation of the person giving evidence is potentially in jeopardy as a result of such investigation. This right was emphasised in *Re the Commission to Inquire into Child Abuse; the Commission v Notice Party A* [2002] 3 I.R. 459. There, the court found that a restriction on the number of legal representatives accompanying a witness before the Commission, to one barrister and one solicitor only, infringed the witness's constitutional right to be represented by counsel of his choice. The Commission could not, on its own initiative, curtail the attendance of the legal representatives of the witness's choosing.

Free legal aid. The key barrier to court access, however, is arguably not legal but financial. Court cases tend to be extremely expensive. Thus the question arises whether a person has a constitutional right to free legal aid in taking a case.

It is clear that free legal aid is certainly required in criminal cases for those who cannot afford legal representation, this being an aspect of the accused's right to defend himself adequately. In *State (Healy) v Donoghue* [1976] I.R. 325, the Supreme Court ruled that a poorly educated and deprived young man was entitled under the Constitution to free legal aid in his defence against charges of criminal wrong-doing. Without such aid, the court reasoned, the accused might well be denied his constitutional right to legal representation at trial, and to mount an adequate defence of his innocence.

Legislation permits those accused of a crime and persons taking family law proceedings to obtain free legal aid from the State, subject to their satisfying the State that they cannot otherwise afford legal representation.

The view that there is no *constitutional* right to free legal aid in civil cases has gradually been eroded. In *O'Shaughnessy v Attorney General* unreported, High Court, February 16, 1971, and *M.C. v Legal Aid Board* [1991] 2 I.R. 43, the courts initially ruled that the State had no constitutional obligation to support private parties in civil cases, in particular in constitutional challenges.

More recent case law suggest that in appropriate civil cases the right to litigate may demand a constitutional right to civil legal aid, at least where the litigant cannot afford legal representation. In *Stevenson v Landy & others* unreported, High Court, Lardner J., February 10, 1993, the High Court ruled that a litigant without sufficient means had a constitutional right to civil legal aid in wardship proceedings. Similarly in *Kirwan v Minister for Justice* [1994] 2 I.R. 417, a person seeking release from the Central Mental Hospital was granted civil legal aid as he could not afford legal representation before a panel considering whether to permit his release. As he lacked the means to collect the relevant information and to formulate and present his case, the Constitution required that he be afforded civil legal aid.

In *O'Donoghue v Legal Aid Board* [2004] I.E.H.C. 413, Kelly J. concluded that a litigant, entitled to legal aid under legislation, had a constitutional entitlement of reasonably prompt access to the courts, which right had been breached by reason of a 25-month delay in gaining access to legal aid. Similarly in *Magee v Farrell* [2005] I.E.H.C. 388, Gilligan J. ruled that fair procedures under the Constitution required that a mother be provided with legal aid for the purpose of being adequately represented at an inquest into her son's death.

The right to travel

In *State (M.) v Attorney General* [1979] I.R. 73, the High Court ruled that a law preventing the removal of certain children from the State, even with the consent of both parents, was unconstitutional. The denial of a passport in this case to an Irish-born infant (whose parents wanted her to travel to live with her grandparents in Nigeria) infringed the girl's constitutional right to travel outside the State.

Similarly, in *Lennon and Ganly v Fitzgerald* [1981] I.L.R.M 84, O'Hanlon J. declined to prevent the Irish rugby union team from travelling to South Africa in the apartheid era, reasoning that to do so would infringe the constitutional right to travel.

It is worth noting in this context the provisions of the Thirteenth Amendment to the Constitution 1992. Under this Amendment women enjoy an express constitutional right to travel to another state where the purpose of such travel is to obtain an abortion, in circumstances where the abortion is legally available in that other State.

The right to communicate

In *Attorney General v Paperlink* [1984] I.L.R.M. 373, Costello J. ruled that citizens have a constitutional right to communicate ideas and information. In *Kearney v Minister for Justice* [1986] I.R. 116, for instance, the High Court ruled that a consistent failure to deliver letters to a prisoner constituted a breach of his right to communicate. Since *Murphy v I.R.T.C.* [1998] 2 I.L.R.M. 360 it is likely that this right will be treated also as an aspect of the right to free expression (see Ch.18 below).

In *Holland v Governor of Portlaoise Prison* [2004] 2 I.R. 573, McKechnie J. declared invalid a decision of the prison governor refusing a prisoner permission to be visited by members of the media. The prisoner in question, the plaintiff, was seeking public support for his claim that he had been wrongly convicted. The prison governor, however, applied a blanket policy that prevented contact between any prisoner and a member of the media. While acknowledging that there might be good reason to limit such access in specific cases, McKechnie J. ruled that the imposition of a blanket ban on media contact disproportionately infringed the right of the prisoner to communicate, as well as his freedom of expression. The judge ruled that the governor was required to consider each request for contact on its merits. He could only restrict contact, moreover, where this was necessary to safeguard the security and good order of the prison.

The right to die a natural death

A person generally has the right to refuse medical treatment or surgery, however necessary it may be, even if this results in the death of that person (see *Re a Ward of Court* [1996] 2 I.R. 79). Ordinarily, where a person is forced to undergo medical treatment against their will, this would amount to a breach of that person's rights to privacy and bodily integrity. In *Re a Ward of Court* [1996] 2 I.R. 79, this right was extended to its logical conclusion, with the Supreme Court ruling that citizens generally have a right to die a natural death. That case involved a woman who had remained in a near-persistent vegetative state for nearly 23 years. She had no control over her bodily movements and had suffered severe brain damage. Her family, distressed at their relative's condition, wanted a tube supplying food to her stomach to be removed, so that she could, as they saw it, die with dignity.

The Supreme Court agreed that a person has the right to refuse such medical treatment even if this resulted in the death of the individual. Where an individual did not, moreover, have the mental capacity to make such a decision, the court itself would decide based on the "best interests" of the person. This does not, however, permit a person actively to take his own life, or another's life. The constitutional right is confined to death by natural means. A person may request the withdrawal of treatment and thus allow nature to take its course, even if this leads to death. There is, however, no constitutional right to die by artificial means, or through the active intervention of another party.

Fair procedures

The courts have concluded on a number of occasions that Art.40.3 entitles citizens to be treated fairly by the State. In particular, it is well established that citizens have a right to have fair procedures (sometimes called "natural justice" or "constitutional justice") applied by state bodies making decisions that impact on citizens. (See *Glover v BLN Ltd.* [1973] I.R. 388, *Garvey v Ireland* [1981] I.R. 75). For instance, in *Maguire v Ardagh* [2002] 1 I.R. 385, the Supreme Court held that a rule restricting the right to cross-examine witnesses before an Oireachtas sub-committee was unconstitutional. The sub-committee was established to inquire into the circumstances of the shooting (allegedly by Gardaí) of John Carthy in Abbeylara, in 2000. Gardaí called to testify before the sub-committee were permitted to cross-examine witnesses only at the end of the sub-committee's oral hearings, and then subject to the approval of the sub-committee. The Supreme Court concluded that this approach did not meet the constitutional requirement of fair standards and was thus unconstitutional.

Some of the key principles of natural justice include:

- **Audi alteram partem:** Both sides have an equal right to have their case heard ('hear both sides'). This includes a right to cross-examine witnesses and to test evidence presented to a court or other decision-making body.
- **Nemo iudex in causa sua:** "A person may not be a judge in her own cause". The decision-maker is required to be independent, impartial and unbiased.
- **Legal representation.** A person has a right to legal representation before a public body where one's right to liberty, property or good name are at stake.
- **Unreasonable decisions:** A decision will not be upheld if it is manifestly unreasonable in that there is no material on which it could have been based or it plainly and unambiguously defies fundamental reason and common sense.
- **Irrelevant considerations.** All relevant considerations should be taken into account and all irrelevant considerations ignored.

No constitutional right is absolute

No constitutional right is ever absolute. Every right is subject to limitations and qualifications, whether on the grounds that the right conflicts with another person's superior rights or that the common good demands that one's rights be curtailed.

The Constitution necessarily permits individual constitutional rights to be limited by reference to certain social or economic priorities and, in particular, by reference to the "common good". The phrase "common good" refers to the collective interest of society as a whole to which the State must look in framing its laws. The Preamble to the Constitution, for instance, while guaranteeing the "dignity and freedom of the individual" insists also that "true social order [be] attained". Similarly, the rights to free expression and association in Art.40.6 are expressly stated to be subject to limitation where "public order or morality" so demand.

Thus, for instance, in *Murray v Ireland* [1985] I.R. 332, [1991] 1 I.L.R.M. 465, the High Court and Supreme Court alike ruled that a married couple's right to have children could be limited in certain cases. The husband and wife in this case were both serving prison sentences for the unlawful killing of a Garda. Although the courts accepted that the couple had a right to bear children, the requirements of prison security, and the duty to safeguard the general public, justified the refusal to facilitate the plaintiffs' aspirations to procreate. Similarly in *Kearney v Minister for Justice* [1986] I.R. 116, the High Court ruled that a prisoner's right to privacy could be curtailed with a view to preventing contraband entering a prison. The prisoner in this case had unsuccessfully challenged the prison authority's actions in opening and scrutinising his mail. The nub of these cases is that while prisoners continue to enjoy constitutional rights, even while incarcerated, such rights are necessarily limited to those consistent with good order and the security of the prison.

The conflicting rights of other persons may be used to justify the curtailment of lesser rights in certain situations. For instance in *People (DPP) v Shaw* [1982] I.R. 1, the Supreme Court ruled that an accused's right to liberty could be curtailed with a view to vindicating the right to life of a young woman. The Gardaí in this case had illegally detained the accused for longer than was permitted by law. This technically meant that a confession he gave while under illegal detention could not be used in evidence against him in his subsequent trial. The court, however, ruled that the "admission" (introduction and consideration during trial) of that evidence had been legally permissible. The accused was detained for longer than permitted simply because the Gardaí felt that he would, if detained, lead them to the whereabouts of a kidnapped woman. The Gardaí honestly believed that the woman was still alive and that the accused could help locate her, thus potentially saving the woman's life. This concern to vindicate the right to life of the kidnapped woman (although she was in fact dead at the time of the accused's arrest) justified in law the curtailment of the accused's right to liberty.

The Constitution itself clearly stipulates that certain rights are subject to limitation. Thus for instance, the right to free expression (in Art.40.6) is said to be subject to the requirement that the organs of public opinion "not be used to undermine public order or morality or the authority of the State". Similarly, the right to life of the unborn child in Art.40.3.3° is expressly stated to be subject to the equal right to life of its mother. Thus, in *Attorney General v X*. [1992] 1 I.R. 1, the Supreme Court ruled that a 14-year-old girl, pregnant by rape, could legally have an abortion in circumstances where she was suicidal. The court reasoned that where there was a "real and substantial risk to the life of the mother", an abortion would be legally permitted under the Constitution, even though this necessarily undermined the right to life of the unborn.

The courts, in asserting the rights of citizens, are in essence involved in a fine balancing act between competing rights and interests. Unfettered liberty is a sure-fire recipe for social upheaval. Thus, the Constitution is careful to underline that as well as enjoying rights, citizens owe duties to the State and to their fellow citizens (see for instance Art.9.3).

The principle of proportionality

As noted above, there are few if any rights recognised by the Constitution as absolute. A key principle in considering the extent to which a right may be curtailed is the principle of proportionality. In many cases, rights may be validly curtailed with a view to achieving a legitimate state purpose. Nonetheless, the courts have consistently noted that the steps taken to achieve this purpose should be no more restrictive than is necessary to achieve the purpose. In other words the measure should "intrude into constitutional rights as little as is reasonably possible" (in *Re Article 26 and the Employment Equality Bill 1996* [1997] 2 I.R. 321). A colloquial way of putting this might be to say that one need not use a sledgehammer to crack a nut.

The permitted severity of the restriction on constitutional rights will necessarily depend on the importance and urgency of the objective behind such a restriction. For instance, the State might very reasonably be permitted to force medical treatment on a person with a severely contagious and ravagingly dangerous virus (such as the Ebola virus); the serious health implications would clearly merit the breach of the patient's bodily integrity. A similar approach obviously would not be justified where the health implications were less severe.

In *Heaney v Ireland* [1994] 3 I.R. 593 (a case concerning permitted restrictions on the right to silence), a proportionality test was set out. First the objective (or reason) behind the restrictive measure must be "of sufficient importance to warrant over-riding a constitutionally protected right." The reasons for the steps must be "pressing and substantial". The restrictions must, moreover, be proportionate in that they: (1) "are rationally connected to the objective...; (2) are not arbitrary, unfair or based on irrational considerations; (3) impair the right as little as possible and (4) their effects on rights are proportional to the objective."

Two examples might be given. In *Cox v Ireland* [1992] 2 I.R. 503, the Supreme Court considered a provision of the Offences Against the State Act 1939 which prevented a person convicted under the Act from working in the public service for seven years thereafter. Deeming this to be unconstitutional, the Supreme Court concluded that the penalty was excessively severe. The plaintiff in that case had been convicted of a relative minor infraction under the Act, but nonetheless lost his job as a teacher, a result that, the court felt, far outweighed the legitimate state interest behind the measure. It thus breached the plaintiff's property rights as well as his right to earn a livelihood.

Similarly, in *Daly v Revenue Commissioners* [1995] 3 I.R. 1, Costello J. struck down a measure preventing self-assessed taxpayers who had paid tax at source from claiming credit for such payments in the same tax year. Credit would only be given in respect of a tax liability for the year *following* the year when the tax was actually paid. Thus, a taxpayer who in 1996 paid tax at source on income would only receive credit against his overall tax liability in respect of his income from 1997. This caused hardship to the taxpayer, the effect being to overcharge the taxpayer but delay repayment by a year. This unfairness was not justified by the purpose of the legislation, which was effectively to manage a transition to a new basis for collecting taxes.

By contrast, in *Heaney v Ireland* restrictions on the right to silence, requiring that an accused account for his movements, were proportionately justified by the State's legitimate interest in tackling serious crime. Similarly in *Murphy v I.R.T.C.* [1999] 1 I.R. 12 restrictions on religious advertising were deemed to be justified by the common good. Religion being a very intimate and divisive issue, the State was entitled to take the view that advertisements promoting a particular religious viewpoint might stir up unrest and resentment. In *Re Article 26 and Part V of the Planning and Development Bill 1999* [2000] 2 I.R. 321, the Supreme Court upheld obligations on property developers to set aside 20 per cent of their land for social and affordable housing. This measure, while restrictive of property rights, was justified by the public interest in providing appropriate accommodation to economically disadvantaged citizens.

Quinn's Supermarket v Attorney General [1972] I.R. 1 offers a further example of the operation of proportionality, this time in balancing different constitutional values. Here, the Supreme Court ruled that the State could discriminate in favour of a particular religious community if such action was necessary to uphold their right to practice their religion. In this case however, a blanket exemption of kosher shops from shop closing regulations was deemed unconstitutional as it went much further than was necessary to achieve the objective of protecting the free practice of religion. (See below at p.187).

17. THE RIGHT TO LIFE

Arguably the most important right in the Constitution, the right to life is guaranteed protection generally by Art.40.3.2°. In the case of the unborn child, moreover, Art.40.3.3° guarantees special protection, subject to the equal right to life of the child's mother.

Of course, the right to life of each individual is subject to the right to life of every other individual. Thus, Irish criminal law acknowledges that a homicide may be justified on the grounds that one person killed another person in self-defence (see the *People (Attorney General) v Dwyer* [1972] I.R. 416).

The ban on the death penalty

The death penalty was abolished in Ireland in 1990 (Criminal Justice Act 1990). Since 2001, moreover, the Constitution contains an express prohibition on the reintroduction of what is sometimes called a "capital offence", an offence punishable by the death of the offender. Article 15.5.2° prevents the Oireachtas from ever prescribing death as a penalty for an offence, even in times of war or emergency. Even if the Oireachtas were to invoke the terms of Art.28.3, exempting a piece of emergency legislation from the requirements of the Constitution, it would still be impossible to prescribe such a penalty.

Abortion and the right to life

The Eighth Amendment to the Constitution 1983 inserted a new Art.40.3.3° into the Constitution. This provision expressly guarantees the "right to life of the unborn child", subject to the equal right to life of its mother.

What is an "unborn child" for this purpose?

The protection afforded by Art.40.3.3 applies only to a foetus from the point of implantation in his or her mother's womb. In other words, an "unborn child" means a child in the womb and not an embryo existing outside the womb. In *M.R. v T.R.* [2006] I.E.H.C. 359, the High Court ruled that embryos created and stored outside the womb do not attract the protection of the Eighth Amendment. Having considered the context against which the Eighth Amendment was passed, McGovern

J. concluded that Art.40.3.3 was designed only to prevent termination of an existing pregnancy (removing the foetus from the womb) and did not prevent the destruction of an embryo which had not yet been placed in the womb. This means, for instance, that embryos outside the womb created for the purpose of research, or for fertility treatment are not constitutionally considered to be "unborn children".

Abortion and the risk of suicide

Effectively Art.40.3.3 bans abortion in Ireland except where the life of the mother is in danger. In *Attorney General v X.* [1992] 1 I.R. 1, the Supreme Court ruled that an abortion would only be legal in Ireland where there was a "real and substantial risk to the life of the mother" necessitating the termination of a pregnancy. The defendant in this case, a 14-year-old girl, had become pregnant by an act of rape. This appalling situation had so affected her that she was rendered suicidal. Although the High Court had imposed an injunction preventing her from travelling to the UK for an abortion, the Supreme Court lifted this injunction. It agreed that the likelihood that the girl would commit suicide constituted a real and substantial threat to her life. Thus, had the mother sought an abortion in Ireland, the abortion would have been legal. The girl could not, moreover, be prevented from going to the UK for the purpose of obtaining an operation that would have been legal in Ireland.

> The termination of a pregnancy, thus, is permitted in Irish law, but only where the continuation of the pregnancy poses *a real and substantial risk to the life of the mother of the child.*

In *A and B. v Eastern Health Board* [1998] 1 I.R. 464, the High Court upheld an order of the District Court permitting a girl in the care of the State to travel to the UK for an abortion. As in the *X.* case, the girl had become pregnant as a result of rape, and there was a real and substantial risk to the life of the mother as a result of her mental condition. The court thus rejected the claim of the parents of the pregnant girl that the State had no authority to facilitate their daughter in travelling for an abortion. This suggests that where the conditions laid down in the *X.* case are satisfied, the State may assist children in its care, even if this results in an abortion.

A more difficult situation arose in *D. v Health Service Executive (HSE)* unreported, McKechnie J., May 9, 2007, which again involved a pregnant child in the care of the State. The girl in this case wished to travel to the UK for an abortion, but was prevented from doing so by the HSE. By contrast with earlier cases, here there was no risk to the life of the mother (and no suggestion of rape). While the mother initially was happy to go ahead with the pregnancy, she later learned that the child, if born alive, tragically had next to no chance of survival due to a condition known as anencephaly, preventing the development of the child's head. (Such children may survive, at most, only a few days outside the womb). While the High Court ruled that the HSE had no authority to prevent the girl from travelling to the UK for an abortion, it must be noted that there would have been no right to have an abortion in this State, notwithstanding the exceptionally limited prospects of the unborn child.

The hierarchy of rights: abortion and the right to travel and to information

It was once believed that the right-to-life amendment could be used to prevent a woman from travelling abroad for an abortion, even to a country where abortion was legal. Whether this was so or not, it was certainly possible to invoke the Eighth Amendment to prevent information on abortion from being distributed in this State. See for instance *Attorney General (S.P.U.C.) v Open Door Counselling* [1988] I.R. 593, *S.P.U.C. v Coogan* [1989] I.R. 734, and *S.P.U.C. v Grogan* [1989] I.R. 753, where the Supreme Court found that the ban on abortion also precluded the distribution of any information that might facilitate an abortion. The argument accepted in these cases was that the right to life prevailed over the right to information such that the distribution of information could be curtailed so as to protect the right to life of the unborn. Similarly, it was suggested by the *X.* case that had the proposed abortion been illegal in Ireland, the mother's right to travel might have been curtailed. Indeed, the High Court had injuncted the mother from travelling before its ruling was successfully appealed to the Supreme Court.

The Thirteenth and Fourteenth Amendments, passed in 1992, now prevent Art.40.3.3 from being used to prevent, respectively, the right to travel and the dissemination of information on abortion. The Thirteenth Amendment prevents the right to life of the unborn child from being invoked to prevent a woman travelling to another State for the purpose of an abortion (where the abortion is legal in that other State). In *D. v Health Service Executive*, for instance, the High Court concluded that the Health Service Executive had no authority to prevent a 17-year-old girl in its care from travelling to the UK for an abortion. Affirming the girl's right to travel, the court ruled that this right existed whether or not the abortion would have been legal in Ireland.

In *A and B. v Eastern Health Board* [1998] 1 I.R. 464, however, the court noted (obiter) that this did not create a right as such, but rather prevented the State from restricting travel in such cases. Nonetheless, the court upheld the decision of the District Court judge in that case to allow the health board to make arrangements for a suicidal pregnant girl in its care to travel for an abortion in the UK.

The Fourteenth Amendment precludes the use of Art.40.3.3° to restrict the availability of information on abortion, e.g. on the contact details of abortion clinics in the UK. (But see also the Regulation of Information Act 1995.)

Suicide and the threat to the mother's life

On two occasions, the State has unsuccessfully sought to amend the Constitution to restrict a mother's right to an abortion where the risk to her life emanates from a mental condition that renders her suicidal. In 1992, the Twelfth Amendment purporting to confine the right to an abortion to cases where the risk did not arise from the mother's suicidal state was rejected in referendum. In 2002, a further amendment (the Twenty-Fifth Amendment) was put to the People in a referendum proposing certain changes to the law on abortion. The referendum suggested that the Constitution would be changed to allow the creation of legislation permitting an abortion where there is a real and substantial risk to the life of the mother but not permitting it in cases where the risk arose from the prospect of the child's mother committing suicide. The referendum was, however, defeated by a narrow margin. This being the case, the law remains as outlined in the *X.* case.

18. FREEDOM OF EXPRESSION

A person generally has the right freely to express his or her convictions or opinions. The State, in other words, is not generally entitled to penalise a person for speaking his or her mind.

While this right, for some time, remained relatively under-developed, the courts in recent years have emphasised the importance of the right of free expression. Encompassed in this right is the concept of the "freedom of the press", the right of media organs to communicate and comment on certain phenomena, in particular those relating to the formation of government policy. The freedom of the press has been emphasised for instance in the *Irish Times v Ireland* [1998] 1 I.R. 359. This case concerned the permissible limits on the requirement that justice be administered in public, the presiding judge having excluded contemporaneous media reporting of a criminal trial. While acknowledging that restrictions could be permitted in order to protect the accused's right to a fair trial, the Supreme Court ruled that the facts of the case did not justify a restriction on publicity in this case. In the course of their judgments, three of the Supreme Court judges referred to the importance of a free press under Art.40.6. Similarly in *Foley v Sunday Newspapers Ltd.* [2005] 1 I.R. 89 Kelly J. endorsed the view that a free press "is an important right and one which the courts must be extremely circumspect about curtailing".

The right of free expression is not, however, confined to the media, but extends to every citizen. In a decision handed down March 15, 2007 (see Carolan, "Court challenge to begging law succeeds", *Irish Times*, March 16, 2007), DeValera J. struck down as unconstitutional a provision of the Vagrancy Act 1847, which penalised the act of begging in public. The judge agreed that the measure in question disproportionately interfered with the accused's right to free expression and his right to communicate.

Freedom of expression also formed the basis for the decision in *Holland v Governor of Portlaoise Prison* [2004] 2 I.R. 573. There McKechnie J. declared invalid a ruling of the prison governor refusing permission to a prisoner seeking approval for visits by members of the media. The prisoner in question, the plaintiff, was seeking public support for his claim that he had been wrongly convicted. The prison governor, however, applied a blanket policy that prevented contact between any prisoner and a member of the media. While acknowledging that free speech was not an absolute right, and might validly be restricted for the purpose of preserving good order in a prison, McKechnie J. ruled that the imposition of a blanket ban on media contact disproportionately infringed the prisoner's right to communicate as well as his freedom of expression. The judge ruled that the governor was required to consider each request for contact on its merits, and that he could only restrict contact where this was necessary to safeguard the security and good order of the prison. In so ruling, McKechnie J. placed particular emphasis on the reason the plaintiff had sought access to the media, being his claim that he was the victim of a miscarriage of justice: where the liberty of a potentially innocent person depends on it, it would be difficult to justify limiting freedom of speech.

Freedom of expression defined

The expression of opinions v dissemination of facts

It was formerly thought that freedom of expression only protected the expression of opinions (what one believes) rather than the dissemination or communication of facts (see, for instance, *Attorney General v Paperlink* [1984] I.L.R.M. 373). In *Murphy v Independent Radio and Television Commission* [1998] 2 I.L.R.M. 360, however, the Supreme Court acknowledged that freedom of expression does indeed extend to the dissemination of facts in the broader sense. This point had earlier been made in *Irish Times v Ireland* [1998] 1 I.R. 359 where Barrington J. observed that the press had a right not only to comment on the news but also a right to report facts on which such opinions might be based. "A constitutional right," he observed, "to comment on the news but not to report it would appear to me to be a nonsense". There is thus a right in Art.40.6 not merely to comment on a state of affairs but also to communicate facts, whether or not the information is accompanied by opinion. In *Holland,* similarly, the High Court relied on both Art.40.3 and Art.40.6.1 and both the right to communicate and to free expression as grounds for its decision, rendering the distinctions between these rights and their sources largely irrelevant for the purpose of the court's decision.

It is said also that from freedom of expression arises a corollary right to silence, that is a right of an accused person *not* to have to convey certain facts to the Gardaí (see *Heaney v Ireland* [1994] 3 I.R. 593, [1996] 1 I.R. 580).

The right to criticise the Government

The Constitution expressly reserves to the citizen the right to criticise his or her Government. It is important in this context, however, to distinguish between speech that criticises the Government and that which seeks to undermine the authority of the State.

The Constitution is also clear in that it guarantees the "rightful liberty" of the media, including the press and cinema, to free expression, and, in particular, the right to criticise Government policy. This right, however, is not unlimited. The Constitution declares, for instance, that the freedom of the press "shall not be used to undermine public order or morality or the authority of the State".

The limits of freedom of expression

Freedom of expression is not absolute. There are limitations upon its exercise that reflect the delicate balance between leaving persons free to speak their mind, and protecting the public against speech that may undermine public security, order or morality.

The Constitution generally reflects the preference that rights be balanced against the interests of the community as a whole, the common good. Article 40.6, which guarantees freedom of expression and free association, expressly states that the exercise of these rights is "subject to public order and morality". Thus, in several respects the constitutional right to free expression has been qualified by the superseding interests of the State and the conflicting rights of other persons. The circumstances in which such restrictions apply can roughly be summarised under the following five headings:

- public morality;
- public order;
- the security of the state;
- respect for the court process; and
- respect for individual rights.

Public morality

Many states limit the right to free expression with a view to upholding general standards of morality. For instance, the Constitution expressly renders illegal "the publication or utterance of blasphemous, seditious or indecent matter". Thus it is perfectly constitutional to censor print publications, films or videos that are deemed to be indecent or obscene, provided always that such measures are proportionate. The Censorship of Films Acts 1923–1992, for example, prohibit any film from being shown in public where it is found to be "indecent, obscene or blasphemous" or if its showing would tend to undermine standards of public morality.

Public order

The law generally prohibits speech that is likely to incite a breach of the peace or otherwise to incite others to commit a crime. In particular, s.6 of the Criminal Justice (Public Order) Act 1994 makes it an offence to use "threatening, abusive or insulting words" in a public place where such words are intended (and likely) to give rise to a breach of the peace.

The security of the State

It is generally constitutional to restrict "seditious" speech, or speech that is otherwise liable to undermine the authority or security of the State. In *State (Lynch) v Cooney* [1983] I.L.R.M. 89 for instance, the Supreme Court had to consider a Government order under s.31 of the Broadcasting Act 1960 banning members of Sinn Féin from being interviewed on Irish radio or television. The court concluded that both s.31 and the specific order in respect of Sinn Féin were constitutional, as they were both considered to be necessary in order to protect the order and authority of the State.

Respect for the court process

While freedom of expression generally allows citizens to criticise the courts, it is illegal to pour scorn on the courts in a manner that brings judges into disrepute. This is called "scandalising" the court. Where a person, for instance, suggests that a judge has behaved illegally or improperly, it is open to the court to find that person in "contempt of court" for such comments.

Example: In *Re Kennedy and McCann* [1976] I.R. 382, a newspaper editor and journalist were fined for bringing a court into contempt. They had suggested that a court considering a custody case had been motivated in its decision more by the wealth and status of certain family members than by the best interests of the child in that case. This allegation, the court found, was likely to bring the court system into disrepute.

Sub judice rules. Again, despite the right to free expression, certain sub judice rules apply, which prevent media outlets from commenting on the proceedings of a pending court case in a manner that may obstruct or otherwise influence the decision in that case. In particular, any comments that might undermine an accused's chances of a fair trial, that suggest for instance that he is guilty of the offence with which he is charged, would be in breach of the sub judice rule. In such circumstances, the publisher of these comments may be liable to be found in contempt of court and in rare conditions a trial might even be suspended or cancelled because of such remarks.

Respect for individual rights

While the Constitution expressly guarantees the freedom of expression of the individual, it also contains an express guarantee of the right to one's good name (Art.40.3.2°). It is thus necessary to balance the right to free speech against the right of an individual not to be "defamed". Thus the law regards libel and slander, collectively known as "defamation", as "torts" or civil wrongs. A comment is said to be defamatory if it cannot be shown to be true and if it tends to bring the person in respect of whom it was made into "public odium and contempt". Similarly, it is not unconstitutional to restrict free speech where the privacy of an individual might otherwise be undermined.

Blasphemy

Uniquely, the Constitution expressly stipulates that the publication or utterance of blasphemous, seditious or indecent matter shall be a criminal offence. While the legislative provisions noted above address the last two of these concerns, there is no legislation in respect of blasphemy.

Blasphemy entails the utterance of comments that are offensive to religious sensibilities. It is one of the few offences that is itself given constitutional status: the Constitution expressly requires that blasphemy be treated as an offence. Nonetheless there is great debate and not a little confusion over what exactly constitutes blasphemy for this purpose. In *Corway v Independent Newspapers* [2000] 1 I.L.R.M. 426, the Supreme Court essentially concluded that there was no workable definition of "blasphemy" that could be applied in these cases. The particular difficulty was that the common law of blasphemy was directed only to the protection of the beliefs of the formerly established Church of Ireland. The Oireachtas had not legislated in this context. In the absence of legislation, the court had no way of enforcing blasphemy rules in a manner that respected the constitutional principle that all religious perspectives be treated equally. This leaves the law concerning blasphemy, and the constitutional requirement that blasphemy be discouraged, in an extremely awkward position.

19. FREEDOM OF ASSOCIATION

The State is generally not entitled to restrain people from associating together or forming unions or associations based on a common interest or concern. By the same token, the State is generally precluded from *forcing* individuals to be part of an organisation of which those individuals disapprove.

The right to form associations v the right to join associations

That is not to say that one has a right to *join* any association. It is, indeed, generally open to a private association or union to exclude persons for whatever reason it considers proper.

Example: In *Tierney v Amalgamated Society of Woodworkers* [1959] I.R. 254, the Supreme Court rejected the contention that the defendant, a craft union, could be forced to accept the plaintiff, an allegedly underqualified carpenter, as a member. It concluded that freedom of association entailed that the defendant, as a voluntary organisation, had the right to accept and reject potential members as it saw fit.

It would, however, be unconstitutional to refuse to allow a person to join a union where such a refusal constituted a "breach of a monopoly position". For instance, in *Murphy v Stewart* [1973] I.R. 97, Walsh J. suggested that where the right to work in a particular place or sector was reserved to members of one union or organisation alone, an unjustifiable refusal to allow a person to join that union might constitute a breach of the constitutional right to earn a livelihood (see above at pp.137–139).

The latter point illustrates that freedom of association is not absolute. The State may curtail such freedom where the curtailment is necessitated by considerations of public order or morality. For example, the Supreme Court in *Norris v Attorney General* [1984] I.R. 36 noted that the right to associate with other persons was limited in that it did not privilege association for the purpose of engaging in homosexual sexual acts.

Notably, the Employment Equality Acts 1998–2004 prevent exclusion from certain voluntary organisations (including trade unions and organizations representing the professions) on specified grounds. It would, for instance, be illegal to exclude a woman from a union on the grounds of her gender, or (under the Equal Status Acts 2000–2004) to refuse to allow a child to join a sports club on account of her race or colour. These restrictions appear, implicitly, to be justified by the legitimate state interest to promote equality and social cohesion, notwithstanding the restriction on free association that it entails.

The right to dissociate

As a corollary to the right to associate and to form unions, citizens also enjoy a right to dissociate, that is, *not* to be a member of a union or association. The State thus cannot support or condone steps taken to force a person to be a member of a union against his will.

Examples: In *Meskell v C.I.É.* [1973] I.R. 121, the defendant, a State-run transport company, attempted to sack all its workers, readmitting them to employment only on condition that they agreed to join one of four specified unions. The Supreme Court ruled that this infringed the constitutional right of the plaintiff not to be a member of a union, i.e. to dissociate.

Similarly, in the *Educational Co. v Fitzpatrick (No. 2)* [1961] I.R. 345, the Supreme Court restrained a picket that had been placed on the plaintiff's business. The picket sought to force the plaintiff to employ only union staff. The court found that as such industrial action sought to undermine the right to dissociate of the employees, the picket was illegal and could thus be restrained.

These cases establish that where industrial action is taken to force union membership on employees, such action is illegal, as it seeks to undermine a constitutional right. The State cannot, for instance, permit a strike (by granting the picketers immunity from suit), as the picket is in furtherance of an unlawful trade dispute, i.e. one undertaken with the purpose of undermining the constitutional right to dissociate from associations or unions. In this context, the *Educational Co.* case and *Cotter v Ahern* [1975–1976] I.L.R.M. 248 suggest that there may in fact be a positive duty on employers and unions to respect employees' constitutional rights.

Union recognition: the right to negotiate?

No employer can be forced to recognise any union or any particular union as being entitled to represent workers in negotiations. It is well within the rights of any employer to refuse generally (as part of their right to dissociate) to negotiate with any trade union or with particular unions. An employer may, for instance, confine its recognition to a small number of approved unions because it fears that a proliferation of unions may make it more difficult to obtain agreement on certain work practices. The Constitution does not impose any obligation on an employer to negotiate with unions in general or with a particular union.

Example: In the *Association of General Practitioners v Minister for Health* [1995] 1 I.R. 382, the High Court ruled that the Minister was not obliged to recognise or negotiate with the plaintiff on behalf of its members. The Minister had already recognised several doctors' representative organisations for this purpose and felt that he should not have to negotiate with another such organisation. (See also *Abbott and Whelan v I.T. & G.W.U.* (1982) 1 J.I.S.L.L. 56).

Restrictions on the right to associate

The right to associate may be qualified by considerations of public order and morality, a point that arguably justifies the banning of various organizations engaged in terrorist activities with a view to undermining the authority or security of the State. Similarly, in *Norris v Attorney General* [1984] I.R. 36 an argument that laws banning homosexual activity (since repealed) infringed the plaintiff's right to associate with other gay men was rejected on the basis that even if it did infringe this right, such infringement was deemed to be justified by considerations of public morality.

The facility to restrict the right to associate is not, however, confined to these grounds. The State may validly restrict the right to associate for other legitimate reasons. In *Portmarnock Golf Club v Ireland* [2005] I.E.H.C. 235, O'Higgins J. in the High Court upheld (obiter) the validity of the Equal Status Act 2000, which potentially prevented clubs from discriminating on various grounds set out in the Act, including gender. The District Court initially concluded that as the club in question permitted only members of the male gender, it was a discriminating club within the meaning of the Act, and could thus be denied a club licence entitling it to sell alcohol. On appeal to the High Court (by way of case stated), O'Higgins J. overturned this verdict, concluding that the legislation exempted the club as its principal purpose was to facilitate the specific needs of male golfers.

The judge nonetheless went on (though it was not strictly necessary to do so, given the interpretation of the Act in the club's favour) to reject the contention that the Act, in restricting the activities of some single gender clubs, might infringe the freedom of association. The judge noted, in particular, that the Act did not prevent the members of discriminating clubs from associating with each other. Instead, it restricted discriminating clubs' access to a drinks licence, which is neither a constitutional right nor a matter integral to the principal purpose of the club. In doing so, O'Higgins J. observed that the State had a legitimate interest in promoting the values of equality and non-discrimination across all strands of society. Freedom of association was, in other words, subject not only to public order and morality, but to other constitutional values, such as in this case, equality.

20. THE FAMILY AND EDUCATION

The Family

Articles 41 and 42 guarantee to the "family" certain "inalienable and imprescriptible rights", special rights that cannot (generally) be given away, taken away or lost. The family, in particular, enjoys a right to autonomy, remaining free from government interference outside of exceptional circumstances. It is important to note, however, that the family that is protected by these Articles is exclusively the family based on marriage. Thus, for instance, an unmarried cohabiting couple enjoys no constitutional rights under these Articles, as the parties are not married to each other.

Collective v individual rights

In *Murray v Ireland* [1985] I.R. 532, Costello J. noted that the rights guaranteed by Art.41 are enjoyed collectively by the family and are not to be seen as individual rights of individual family members. That said, it is possible for these rights to be invoked by a family member on behalf of the family as a unit. For instance, in the *DPP v J.T.* (1988) 3 Frewen 141, a mentally disabled girl successfully argued that alleged sexual abuse at the hands of her father constituted a breach of the family's collective right to protection under Art.41 such that the man's wife could not be prevented from testifying against him.

Marriage and the Family

The Constitution sees marriage as the essential foundation of the family. It requires the State "to guard with special care the institution of Marriage ... and to protect it against attack" (Art.41.3.1°).

In *State (Nicolaou) v An Bord Uchtála* [1966] I.R. 567, the Supreme Court ruled that an unmarried father (Mr Nicolaou) and his child were not part of a family recognised by Art.41. The father and mother of the child, though unmarried, had enjoyed a committed relationship for some time before and after their daughter's birth. When the couple split, however, the mother put their child up for adoption without Mr Nicolaou's consent. In response to the father's objection that this infringed his family rights under Art.41, the Supreme Court ruled that the father could not plead any of the rights afforded by Art.41, as he was not a member of a constitutionally recognised family. This outcome derived, the court argued, from the wording of Art.41 itself. In Art.41.3.1° the State pledges to guard with special care the institution of marriage on which, it says, "the Family is founded".

24 years later, in *K. v W.* [1990] 2 I.R. 437, the Supreme Court again reaffirmed the exclusivity of the family recognised by Art.41. The plaintiff in this case was again an unmarried father of a young child who was being put up for adoption by its mother without the father's consent. Again, the father's claim that this breached his constitutional rights under Art.41 was rejected. The father was not, the court reasoned, a member of the type of family envisaged by the Constitution. In both *K. v W.* and *W.O'R. v E.H.* [1996] 2 I.R. 248, the Supreme Court thus reiterated the position first put in *Nicolaou* that, whatever legal rights a father might have, he certainly enjoys no constitutional rights in respect of his child.

"An attack on the institution of marriage"

Generally, then, marriage enjoys a privileged position under the Constitution. It is unconstitutional, for instance, for the State to treat a non-marital family more favourably than one based on marriage. In *Murphy v Attorney General* [1982] I.R. 241, for instance, the Supreme Court struck down certain provisions of the tax code, on the grounds that they potentially placed a higher tax burden on a married couple than on a similarly placed non-marital couple. Similarly, in *Greene v Minister for Agriculture* [1990] 2 I.R. 17, the Supreme Court ruled that a scheme that discriminated in favour of unmarried farmers was unconstitutional. Access to the scheme in question, an EU farm incomes support initiative, was subject to a means test. For this purpose, the off-farm income of a farmer's spouse, but not of a farmer's cohabiting non-marital partner, was to be considered as part of the income of the farmer. This meant that a married farmer might not qualify for farm support in a case where a similarly placed unmarried (but cohabiting) farmer would.

By the same token, this constitutional preference for marriage has been used to justify measures that discriminate against members of the non-marital family. In *O'B. v S.* [1984] I.R. 316, for instance, the plaintiff had claimed that provisions of the Succession Act 1965 were unconstitutional on the grounds that they discriminated against a child of unmarried parents. Under that legislation, a child whose parents had died intestate (without making a will) could only claim from her mother's or father's estate if their parents had been married to each other. While the court agreed that this did constitute discriminatory treatment, it concluded that this differential treatment was constitutionally justified by the provisions of Art.41 in that the discrimination simply endorsed the constitutional preference for marriage. (The legislation has since been amended to equalize the position of non-marital children).

Custody disputes: the presumption in favour of a child's married parents

In custody disputes between the two natural parents of child, whether married or unmarried, the best interests of the child are deemed in law to rank as the primary consideration. Where, however, the dispute is between the married parents of a child and some other person or persons who have custody of the child, the best interests test is qualified. In such cases the court must assume that the child's best interests are generally served by being returned to the custody of the child's original marital family.

This preference for marriage was most heavily underlined in the custody case of *Re J.H.; K.C. v An Bord Uchtála* [1985] I.R. 375. In that case a then unmarried mother had placed her child for adoption. The mother subsequently married the father of the child and requested that the child be returned to them. Because the natural parents were now married, the adoption could not proceed (see below at pp.173– 174). The question that then arose was who would have custody of the child. Because of the length of time during which the child had been living with his prospective adopters, the High Court initially ruled that it was in the best interests of the child that they should retain custody. To do otherwise, the court reasoned, would risk seriously damaging the child's psychiatric wellbeing.

The Supreme Court, however, ruled that in such cases there was a constitutional presumption that the child's best interests lay with its being returned to its constitutional family. This presumption, moreover, could only be displaced by strong countervailing reasons justifying a different conclusion. When this constitutional presumption was applied by the High Court, on reconsideration of the child's custody, Lynch J. reluctantly ruled that the natural and now married parents should have custody of the child. This was despite the fact that the child had spent nearly three years apart from them. It seems here that even the interests of a child can be glossed over in pursuit of the ideological preference for the marital family.

The passage of time has not dented the strength of this presumption. Indeed, the presumption has been reaffirmed by the Supreme Court in *N. and N. v Health Service Executive* [2006] I.E.S.C. 60 (commonly known as the "Baby Ann" case), the facts of which are very similar to those in *J.H.* The parents in this more recent case, having placed their child for adoption, changed their minds before the adoption order was made final. They requested the return of their child. While the natural parents were unmarried at the time the child was initially placed for adoption, they subsequently married each other. By this stage, however, the child had been in the custody of its proposed adoptive parents for some two years, and had bonded with them. Nonetheless, in line with the presumption, the Supreme Court ruled that the courts could only decline to return the child to its married parents' care where there were exceptional circumstances or compelling reasons justifying such a refusal. In this case, while the child had spent two years with its then current custodians, the heavy burden of proving compelling reasons for the refusal to return the child had not been met. In particular, the court was satisfied that the natural parents had not failed in their duty towards the child, and that the return of the child, if carefully managed, would be feasible. Crucially, McGuinness J. highlighted that the intervening marriage of the parents was integral to their success; had they remained unmarried, the presumption would not have applied.

Lone parents and their children

It is not, however, unconstitutional to have regard to certain practical differences between one-parent and two-parent families, in particular, the extra burden that is placed on lone parents by virtue of their situation. In *MhicMhathúna v Ireland* [1995] I.L.R.M. 69, the Supreme Court ruled that special social welfare and tax allowances for lone parents did not constitute an attack on marriage. The court considered that the State was entitled to recognise the more difficult plight of the single parent relative to that of a couple with children.

Limitations on family rights

While family rights enjoy a privileged status in the Constitution, they are not absolute. In *Murray v Ireland* [1991] 1 I.L.R.M. 465, for instance, the Supreme Court ruled that the rights of an imprisoned married couple to conjugal visits while in prison could legitimately be curtailed in the interests of prison security.

In particular, the right to a family life cannot be used absolutely to preclude the State from enforcing immigration law, e.g. by deporting a parent or spouse who is not an EU citizen. In *Osheku v Ireland* [1987] I.L.R.M. 330, the High Court ruled that the fact that the plaintiff, a non-Irish national, was married to an Irish citizen did not prevent his removal from the State. The rights enjoyed by the family, while significant, were not absolute and could be curtailed where this was necessary to achieve the common good. (See also *Pok Sun Shum v Ireland* [1986] I.L.R.M. 593 and *Margine v Minister for Justice, Equality and Law Reform* [2004] I.E.H.C. 127).

The State is, in short, entitled to control entry at its borders and to manage immigration in an orderly fashion, provided always that it acts reasonably and proportionately. It is permitted, moreover, to act so as to preserve the orderly operation of the asylum regime. In *Lobe, Osayande and Others v Minister for Justice, Equality and Law Reform* [2003] 1 I.R. 1, the Supreme Court confirmed that the non-EU national parents of an Irish-citizen child can be removed from the State, even if this has the practical effect of requiring the citizen also to leave. This case concerned an attempt by the State to deport unsuccessful asylum seekers. The plaintiffs were the parents of children who, because of their birth in the State, enjoyed Irish citizenship. Normally, a citizen has a right of residence in the State. The court agreed that the child has a constitutional right to the care and company of other family members, including its parents.

A majority concluded, however, that the common good required that the child's family rights could be curtailed where necessary to uphold the integrity of the State's asylum and immigration systems. The court thus ruled that it is legally and constitutionally possible for the State to deport the non-Irish national parents of an Irish child, if the Minister forms the view that the common good so required. This is permitted notwithstanding the fact that an Irish-born child might also effectively have to leave the State in order to enjoy the continued company of its family.

That is not to say that the Minister may ignore the family rights of citizens in making his or her decisions. The Minister is obliged, in considering a proposal to deport, to give due weight to any family relationships that would be affected by his decision. In sum, however, the simple fact that a constitutional family might be affected is not an absolute bar to deportation. The fact that the Minister is obliged to consider the existence of a family relationship does not ultimately preclude a decision to deport a family member, if otherwise considered appropriate.

N.B. To a large extent, the situation in *Lobe* is now of less relevance given that, as a result of the Twenty-Seventh Amendment, citizenship is no longer automatically conferred on birth. (See above at pp.37–39)

The definition of marriage

The term "marriage", as used in the Constitution, is understood to mean the marriage of one man and one woman, and not two persons of the same sex. In *Zappone and Gilligan v Revenue Commissioners* [2006] I.E.H.C. 404, two women in a long-standing lesbian relationship married in Canada, which permits same-sex marriage. They challenged the refusal of the Revenue Commissioners to recognize them as a married couple for tax purposes. The High Court rejected this challenge. While acknowledging that 'marriage' is undefined in the text of the Constitution, Dunne J. ruled that the constitutional definition of marriage was confined to couples of the opposite sex. Adopting a historicist approach, Dunne J. concluded that the People in 1937 could only have intended the term to mean heterosexual marriage. While the Constitution was an organic document, capable of changing in line with developments in society, Dunne J. did not believe that there was sufficient evidence of a consensus to change the definition of marriage. Indeed the Civil Registration Act 2004 expressly precludes same-sex marriage.

Equality between spouses

In *Re Tilson* [1951] I.R. 1, the Supreme Court ruled that, notwithstanding any contrary rule of law or social practice, a husband and wife are equal in law, in particular in relation to the upbringing of their children. Thus the court held that a father could not depart from an agreement made with his wife regarding the religious upbringing of their children. Similarly, in *State (DPP) v Walsh* [1981] I.R. 412 the Supreme Court had to consider the legality of an old presumption that a wife who commits a crime in the presence of her husband did so under coercion by him. This presumption was unconstitutional, the court ruled, it being inconsistent with the principle that husband and wife were equal in law (see also the cases discussed above at pp.128–129).

The autonomy of the constitutional family

The constitutional family is considered to enjoy a strong measure of independence from government interference. It is said, thus, that the family enjoys a general "autonomy", that is a right to make decisions as to its best interests without being overruled by the State. The State cannot, for instance, tell a family how many children it may (or should) have, or where its children should attend school.

Example: In *McGee v Attorney General* [1974] I.R. 284, a landmark decision of the Supreme Court, legislation prohibiting the sale and importation of contraception was struck down on the grounds that it infringed a married couple's right to limit the size of its family. Ordinarily no person may limit family size by means of abortion, but a married couple is otherwise free to have as many (or as few) children as it pleases.

Example: In *Re Article 26 and the Matrimonial Home Bill 1993* [1994] 1 I.R. 305, the Supreme Court had to consider a Bill that was designed to split the beneficial ownership of the family home of all married couples between the spouses jointly and equally. As in *McGee*, the Supreme Court ruled that such a measure would infringe the autonomy of the family, this time in relation to decisions regarding property. The court felt that the legislation stood to upset long-standing family agreements about the ownership of the matrimonial home in contravention of the family's right to autonomy.

Example: In *North-Western Health Board v H.W.* [2001] 3 I.R. 622, the Supreme Court prevented the State from interfering with the privileges of the marital family. In that case the court ruled that the State could not, without the consent of his parents, perform a relatively simple "pin-prick test" on a child to test for PKU and other biochemical and metabolic disorders. PKU is an illness that, while easily treated, affects a disproportionate number of Irish people, the incidence being high by international standards. This case establishes that except in extreme circumstances, the State cannot generally order that a child undergo medical treatment or testing where its parents object to such treatment.

Example: In *McK v Information Commissioner* [2006] I.E.S.C. 2, the Supreme Court again emphasised the strong constitutional position of married parents, even where they have been separated. The plaintiff's daughter (who was living with other relatives) had been hospitalised with an infection. The father sought, but was refused access to his young daughter's medical records. The Information Commissioner upheld this refusal, concluding that the father had failed to establish that the release of the records would serve the child's best interests.

In quashing this decision, the Supreme Court ruled that there was a presumption, flowing from Arts 41 and 42, that parents should normally be entitled to access information on their child's medical state. While this was not an absolute right, the Information Commissioner was required, in deciding whether to grant access to such information, to have regard to this presumption. The presumption could be rebutted by evidence that it was not in the best interests of the child to release the information. Nonetheless, the Information Commissioner had erred in requiring the father to establish that his access to the records would serve his daughter's best interests. The correct test is to presume that such access is in the child's best interests until the opposite is established. In so ruling, the Supreme Court stressed the importance of the parent-child relationship under the Constitution. (Nonetheless, on the subsequent application of the correct test, it is worth noting that the Information Commissioner still denied the father such access).

Freedom of choice in education

Article 42 is also worthy of note in this context. The provisions of this Article prevent the State from limiting parental choice by instructing parents to send their children to a particular school or type of school. Article 42 states clearly that the primary educator of the child is to be its parents. Thus the parents of a child are afforded considerable freedom in determining how their children are to be educated. For instance, the State is not permitted to instruct parents to send their children to particular schools or types of schools (e.g. State schools as opposed to private schools). Nor can the State force a child to undergo religious education in a school funded by the State (see Art.44.2.4°).

The rights of non-marital parents and families

Families not based on marriage do not enjoy the constitutional rights guaranteed by Art.41. Nevertheless, the courts have found that both unmarried mothers and their children (but not the fathers of such children) enjoy certain personal constitutional rights as a result of Art.40.3.1°.

A child born to unmarried parents enjoys, under Art.40.3.1°, rights similar to those enjoyed by a marital child under Art.42. These rights include the right to the care and custody of his mother (though not, it seems, his father) and the right to an adequate education and upbringing (*Re M., an infant* [1946] I.R. 334).

A mother who is not married to the father of her child also enjoys the constitutional right and duty, under Art.40.3.1°, to care for and have custody of her child (*G. v An Bord Uchtála* [1980] I.R. 32). Under the Guardianship of Infants Act 1964, moreover, the mother is deemed automatically to be the sole guardian of her child, that is, the person who makes most of the important decisions concerning the child's overall general upbringing.

In sharp contrast, a father who is not married to the mother of his child enjoys *no* constitutional rights in respect of that child. The Supreme Court has consistently ruled that while an unmarried father may have certain legal rights, he has no constitutional rights to the care and custody of his child either under Arts 41 or 40.3. (See *State (Nicolaou) v An Bord Uchtála* [1966] I.R. 567, *K. v W.* [1990] 2 I.R. 437 and *W.O'R v E.H.* [1996] 2 I.R. 248). An unmarried father may be made a joint guardian of his child, either by court order or by statutory declaration made voluntarily by the child's mother and father. Otherwise, however, an unmarried father has no *automatic* right to either the guardianship or to the custody (day-to-day care) of his child.

The unmarried father of a child has, moreover, no constitutional right to object to the adoption of his child. A father is statutorily entitled (under the Adoption Act 1998) to be consulted in respect of a proposal to adopt his child, but, in law, he may only veto the adoption if he is a guardian.

Differences between children born inside and outside marriage

Under legislation, a child born outside marriage is generally to be treated the same as a child born inside marriage (Status of Children Act 1987). The Constitution, however, continues to differentiate based on marital status in the legal treatment of such children.

A child born inside marriage *cannot generally be adopted*, even with the consent of its parents. This is because the constitutional rights and duties of marital parents in respect of their children are described in Art.42 as "inalienable" and "imprescriptible". In other words, they cannot be given away, taken away or lost. Article 42.5 and the

Adoption Act 1988 together allow the adoption of marital children, but only where there has been a serious and ongoing abandonment of the child that is likely to continue until the child is at least 18 years of age (see *Re the Adoption Bill 1987* [1989] I.R. 656).

A child born outside marriage, by contrast, is generally eligible for adoption. Provided that its mother (and any other guardian) gives a full, free and informed consent to the adoption (see *G. v An Bord Uchtála* [1980] I.R. 32, *M. v An Bord Uchtála* [1977] I.R. 287), she is entitled to "waive" her right to the care and custody of her child.

All children have *guardians*, that is a person or persons who are required to make the important decisions concerning that child's overall upbringing, for instance, where she goes to school, in what religion (if any) she is to be raised, and whether she should undergo medical treatment. The guardians of a child born inside marriage are both its parents, jointly and equally. With a non-marital child, however, only the mother is automatically deemed to be a guardian. The father may apply to court to be made a guardian, or acquire guardianship by agreement with the mother, but he has no automatic entitlement either to succeed in the court application (see *K. v W.* [1990] 2 I.R. 437) or to gain the mother's consent to a guardianship agreement.

With custody disputes, as in all matters concerning children, the general rule is that the best interests of the child will dictate the result. That said, there is a constitutional presumption that the best interests of a child born inside marriage lie (unless strong countervailing reasons exist) in remaining with his or her natural (and married) parents (see the discussion above at pp.167–168). Although this presumption may be dislodged, it places a very high barrier in the path of persons who wish to gain custody of a child in proceedings taken against its natural married parents. No such presumption, of course, applies to non-marital children, whose best interests prevail regardless of any constitutional provision.

Divorce

Prior to 1995, it was not possible to obtain a divorce from a court in the Republic of Ireland. This was because of the prohibition on divorce in Art.41.3.2°, which prohibition was removed by referendum in November 1995 (the Fifteenth Amendment of the Constitution). Today it is possible to secure a divorce, and thus to remarry, under the terms of the new Art.41.3.2°. This provision requires that a court may only grant a dissolution of marriage where:

- the parties have been living apart for four of the previous five years;
- there is no reasonable prospect of rehabilitation between the parties; and
- the court is satisfied that reasonable provision has been made for both spouses and for any children of the parties.

The requirement of "living apart" presupposes more than mere physical separation. It also requires a mental element, a resolve on the part of one or both parties that the marriage has come to an end. Thus, living apart does not mandate that the parties physically live in separate houses: it is possible for spouses to share the same house and nonetheless to be living apart, provided that they live largely separate lives (see *McA. v McA.* [2000] 2 I.L.R.M. 48).

Article 42 and the education of children

Article 42 acknowledges parents to be the natural and primary educators of their children. The parents to whom this provision applies are, as in Art.41, the parents of children born within marriage.

- Thus married parents have both a right and a duty, "to provide, according to their means, for the religious and moral, intellectual, physical and social education of their children".
- These parental rights and duties are described, moreover, as "inalienable" and "imprescriptible". In other words, they cannot generally be given away, taken away or lost. This means, for instance, that the child of married parents cannot, except in cases of exceptional neglect, be adopted, even with the consent of its parents, because such an adoption would involve the termination of "inalienable" or "imprescriptible" rights and duties.
- The parents of children enjoy freedom of choice in relation to the education of their children. Parents cannot, in particular, be forced to send their children to schools designated by the State.
- The State is, however, entitled to require that children obtain a "certain minimum level [of] education, moral, intellectual and social". Failure to provide "suitable elementary education" for a

child may, indeed, lead to the prosecution of parents as in *DPP v Best* [2000] 2 I.L.R.M. 1.

- Article 42.5 allows the State to step in to take the place of the parents of a child, but only in exceptional cases where those parents have, for moral or physical reasons, failed in their duty towards the child. On this basis, the Adoption Act 1988 allows for the adoption of marital children, although in cases of extreme ongoing neglect only. Similarly, the Child Care Act 1991 (as amended) provides for children to be taken into the care of the State, though the Act regards such steps as permissible only as a last resort where less serious steps have failed.

The right to a free primary education

Article 42.4 obliges the State to provide for free primary education. The right to avail of this, however, is confined to "children", being persons under the age of 18. In *Sinnott v Minister for Education* [2001] 2 I.R. 545, the Supreme Court ruled that a 23-year-old mentally disabled man was not, as a matter of constitutional right, entitled to continuing state provision for his primary education. In doing so, the Supreme Court overruled the High Court decision of Barr J., who had concluded that the right to free primary education lasted for so long as the education was needed by the disabled person.

Article 42.4 does not place any obligation on the State itself to educate children. The language used here is important: the State is essentially obliged to provide *for* such education, in other words to fund its provision by either the State or by private groups. The primary responsibility to educate in this context is that of the parents. The State in this regard is essentially expected to cater for parental choice, in short, to *support and facilitate* the provision of free primary education by funding its delivery. As Kenny J. observed in *Crowley v Ireland* [1980] I.R. 102, the State itself "... is under no obligation to educate". Instead, the State supports and facilitates the delivery of education by parents in their local communities, usually, though not exclusively, acting through their churches. Effectively, then, the State is obliged to "provide the buildings, to pay the teachers...to provide the means of transport to the schools if this is necessary to avoid hardship, and to prescribe minimum standards." This view appears to have been endorsed in *Campaign to Separate Church and State v Minister for Education* [1998] 2 I.L.R.M. 81, where the Supreme Court upheld state funding for religious chaplains in community schools. They did so partly on the basis that the funding was required to vindicate the rights of parents under Art.42.4 to an education of their choice, which education might feasibly include matters of religious and moral formation. In other words, the funding facilitated parental choice.

21. PROPERTY RIGHTS

Articles 40.3.2° and 43 of the Constitution concern the right to own property, and to have that property protected from unjust attack. "Property" in this context includes "real" property (land and that which is attached to or associated with land) as well as "personal" property (moveable goods, and other items not attached to or associated with land). In fact the term "property" has been interpreted quite widely so as to include property of a relatively intangible nature, such as an employment contract or a taxi licence.

It is clear also that a right to litigate for the recovery of money or land may be a property right for these purposes. For instance, in *Re Article 26 and the Health (Amendment) (No. 2) Bill 2004* [2005] I.E.S.C. 7, the Supreme Court ruled that a right to sue to recover monies collected in breach of the law was a property right protected under Art.40.3.

A pension and other entitlements flowing from employment may also give rise to a property right for this purpose. In *Cox v Ireland* [1992] 2 I.R. 503 a measure preventing a convicted person from working for the State was struck down as disproportionate relative to the seriousness of his crime. The section in question also permitted the State to deny the payment of a pension and other annuities to which the plaintiff was entitled on foot of his past employment. This, the court concluded, constituted a disproportionate infringement of the plaintiff's property rights, given the relatively minor nature of the crimes for which he had been convicted. Likewise, *Lovett v Minister for Education* [1997] I.L.R.M. 89 concerned a measure that sought to nullify the pension of a retired teacher on imprisonment for more than 12 months. This, Kelly J. concluded, was disproportionate in that the severe penalty far outstripped the relatively minor nature of some of the crimes to which it was applied. In both cases the courts noted that the offences were not of sufficient seriousness to justify the serious restriction of the plaintiffs' property rights.

The scope (and limits) of property rights

While it is said that Art.43 protects the *general* right to own and transfer property, Art.40.3.2° concerns the *personal* property rights of individuals in respect of *specific* items of property belonging to them.

The distinction is explained by O'Higgins C.J. in *Blake v Attorney General* [1982] I.R. 117, where he noted the following.

- **Article 43** "prohibits the abolition of private property as an institution". In particular, it guarantees the *general* right to pass property by will and to buy and sell property. Thus it would not be possible to prevent *any* private ownership of property, as demanded for instance, by the principles of Marxism (which advocate the public ownership of all property).
- **Article 40.3**, on the other hand, protects "the citizen's right to a particular item of property" belonging or bequeathed to him *in a specific case*.

These rights are not, however, without limits. Article 43.2, for instance, expressly contemplates the limitation of the right to own property where it is necessary to achieve the common good. This means that a property owner's rights may be legally delimited where it is necessary to do so to promote the interests of the community as a whole. The exercise of property rights is said to be subject to regulation in accordance with "the principles of social justice". The State may, thus, "delimit" the exercise of such rights "with a view to reconciling their exercise with the exigencies [requirements] of the common good."

A good example of this is provided by laws requiring planning permission as a prerequisite to building, the common good demanding that any construction not unduly disturb the environmental amenity of an area. (See the Planning and Developments Acts 2000–2002). Likewise, it is open to the State compulsorily to purchase land without the consent of the owner, where such land is necessary for important public projects, e.g. the building of roads. Again, the rationale for the legality of such an infringement of property rights is that the transfer of land is necessary in order to promote the best interests of the community at large.

The right to compensation

Even where the State may legally delimit the exercise of property rights, however, it would ordinarily be unconstitutional to deprive a person of property without compensation for such loss. Although the Constitution *expressly* mentions the right to compensation only in

Art.44.2.6°, where property is being compulsorily purchased from a religious order, it is suggested that the seizure of property without compensation would, in almost every other case, constitute an "unjust attack" on the property rights of the individual (see Art.40.3.2° and below at pp.180–183). This was clearly the view of Kenny J. in *Central Dublin Development Association v Attorney General* (1975) 109 I.L.T.R. 69. There, the learned judge suggested that, as a general rule, State acquisition of the full ownership rights in a property without compensation "would in all cases be such an [unjust] attack". Similarly, in *Re Article 26 and Part V of the Planning and Development Bill 1999* [2000] 2 I.R. 321, Keane C.J. notes that:

> "There can be no doubt that a person who is compulsorily deprived of his or her property in the interests of the common good should normally be fully compensated at a level equivalent to at least the market value of the acquired property."

Outside of exceptional cases, then, the compulsory seizure of a full interest in land cannot legally proceed without compensation being given. Even where a limited interest in land is being taken, moreover, the courts may sometimes demand that compensation be given to prevent an "unjust attack" on the property owner's rights. For instance, in *E.S.B. v Gormley* [1985] I.L.R.M. 494, the Supreme Court ruled that a property owner had to be compensated by the ESB for the routing of large electricity pylons through his land. Although the court agreed that the ESB could undertake this work without the owner's consent (this being necessary to promote the interests of the common good), it concluded that their refusal to compensate the defendant constituted a breach of his property rights.

An "unjust attack" on property rights

While the Constitution does permit limited interference with property rights where the public interest so demands, Art.40.3.2° generally purports to protect these rights from "unjust attack". This means that the property rights of an individual cannot ordinarily be taken away in a manner that is objectively unreasonable, unfairly discriminatory or arbitrary.

The most recent example of an unjust attack on property rights is provided by the Supreme Court decision in *Re Article 26 and the*

Health (Amendment) (No. 2) Bill 2004 [2005] I.E.S.C. 7. Previous legislation gave certain categories of elderly and infirm persons a right to long-term residential care at the expense of the State. In clear breach of this legislation, the State had levied charges on people who were in fact entitled to free care. The 2004 Bill had attempted to prevent these people from suing for recovery of the money paid in breach of the law. The Supreme Court agreed that there was no general constitutional right to free health care, and thus that provisions levying charges on residents prospectively (i.e. for care provided from 2004 onward) were constitutional. It concluded, nonetheless, that the attempt retrospectively to validate the illegal payments made before 2004, preventing people from suing for recovery of that money, constituted an unjust attack on the property rights of the litigants. The court's view was the right to sue to recover monies collected in breach of the law was a property right protected under Art.40.3. As the Bill was attempting to remove this right, it was unconstitutional. While the court acknowledged that this would have an impact on the finances of the State, such an intrusion could only be justified to avoid "extreme financial crisis", which was not the case in this situation.

Example: *Buckley v Attorney General (the "Sinn Féin Funds" case)* [1950] I.R. 67, concerned the ownership of trust monies held in the name of Sinn Féin. In the midst of a court case where the rightful ownership of the monies was being considered, the Oireachtas purported to "settle the case" by legislation. The legislation stated that the case should be terminated and the money distributed in a particular manner. The Supreme Court concluded that the Oireachtas, in so doing, in addition to interfering in the administration of justice, had breached the property rights of the litigants. By its actions, the Oireachtas had removed from the plaintiffs their right to assert ownership of the monies, a chose in action, and ultimately to obtain access to the funds. This constituted a breach of Art.43, there being no legitimate state interest to justify the intrusion in this case.

Example: In *Brennan v Attorney General* [1984] I.L.R.M. 355, Barrington J. ruled that a system for the collection of rates from landowners amounted to an unjust attack on property rights. Notably, the valuations on which these rates were based were in some cases nearly 100 years old and in many cases did not reflect the true modern value of the land to which they applied. Thus, farmers with relatively poor land often found themselves paying far more in rates than farmers with more fertile properties. This being so arbitrary and irrational as to amount to an "unjust attack" on the plaintiff's property rights, the system was struck down as being unconstitutional.

Example: In *Blake v Attorney General* [1982] I.R. 117, the plaintiff challenged the provisions of the Rent Restrictions Acts 1960–1967. These measures were designed broadly to control rental prices and to protect the tenancy rights of people renting designated properties. This legislation applied, moreover, only to properties built before 1941 and not thereafter. In these circumstances, the Supreme Court concluded that the rent controls constituted an unjust attack on property rights. Of special significance was the fact that the legislation arbitrarily distinguished between properties built before and after 1941, with no good reason for so doing.

The legislature's subsequent attempt to repair this injustice ran aground in a roughly similar manner. In the Article 26 reference of the *Housing (Private Rented Dwellings) Bill 1981* [1984] I.L.R.M. 246, the Supreme Court ruled that rent restriction provisions that proposed to phase out rent control over five years were unconstitutional. The legislation proposed that landlords would continue to be deprived of the full open-market value of rent, thus constituting an unjust attack on their property rights.

The net principle from these cases is that while the State may duly limit the property rights of landlords, it must not do so in a manner that either (a) arbitrarily discriminates between similarly placed individuals or (b) unfairly deprives such businesspersons of a fair market value for their product.

The policy of the State in these cases, that a specific segment of society be singled out to fund certain socially desirable outcomes, was again the subject of constitutional challenge in the Article 26 references of the *Employment Equality Bill 1996* [1997] 2 I.R. 321, and the *Equal Status Bill 1997* [1997] 2 I.R. 387. In each of these cases, employers and service providers respectively were called upon to equip their premises to make them fully accessible to people with disabilities. Although this was a worthy aim, the Supreme Court ruled that the requirements placed on employers and businesspersons by this legislation constituted an unjust attack on the property rights of those individuals. By singling out a narrow segment of society to fulfil what is, after all, a general duty of society as a whole, the legislation amounted to an unfairly arbitrary treatment of those persons' property rights.

It seems, however, that the Supreme Court's view in this regard has been qualified heavily by the decision in the Article 26 reference of

Part V of the Planning and Development Bill 1999 [2001] 1 I.L.R.M. 81. That provision, which was upheld as constitutional by the Supreme Court, proposed to require of builders that up to 20 per cent of building development land be set aside for social housing. Arguably this represents a departure from earlier authority, a signal that the courts may be more willing to countenance giving the State greater leeway to curtail the property rights of big business.

22. FREEDOM OF RELIGION

Religious conflict has been a regular feature of our island's history. It was thus a primary concern of those interested in shaping a new Irish State that the State would be one in which persons of all religions (and none) would be equally entitled to participate. To this end, Art.44 broadly grants freedom of religion to the citizens of Ireland. This means that:

- the State cannot force an individual to be a member of a particular religious denomination;
- the State may not generally penalise a person for membership of a particular religion or for not being a member of any religious grouping.

The State, nonetheless, generally supports the practice of religion. Article 44, after all, begins by stating that "the homage of public worship is due to Almighty God" whose Name shall be held "in reverence" (Art.44.1). In fact, it is fair to conclude that the Constitution is not neutral in respect of religion; it very heavily favours support for the promotion of religious values, subject to the principle of non-discrimination.

The establishment and endowment of religion

The State may neither establish nor endow religion. An "establishment" of religion involves making a particular religion the religion of a State. In England and Wales, for instance, the Anglican faith has been established as the official faith of that jurisdiction. There can, by contrast, be no "established" religion in Ireland, such establishment being a clear example of the type of religious discrimination prohibited by Art.44.2.3.

Compare and contrast

The US Supreme Court has decided, based on its freedom of religion guarantee, that in the United States:

- Schools teaching or professing a particular religion cannot receive State funding;

- State-funded schools in the United States may *not* endorse any particular religion;
- The organised recital of prayers is banned in State-funded schools (*Abingdon School District v Schempp* 374 U.S. 203 (1963));
- State-run or funded bodies in the United States may *not* display or fund the display of religious icons or otherwise endorse religious practices (although see *Lynch v Donnelly* 465 U.S. 668 (1984)).

In Ireland, by contrast, the State appears entitled to fund religion in certain respects, provided that it does so in an even-handed manner. Thus the Constitution appears to permit (according to the Supreme Court in *Campaign to Separate Church and State v Minister for Education* [1998] 2 I.L.R.M. 181):

- the general State funding of denominational (religious run) education;
- religious instruction in State-funded schools (subject to the right not to attend such classes);
- State funding for religious instruction in denominational schools;
- State funding for the supply of chaplains to State schools; and
- the display of religious icons (such as crucifixes and religious statues) in State-funded but religious-run hospitals and schools.

The courts, however, are reluctant to involve themselves in disputes between different moral and religious perspectives, preferring to maintain, in their deliberations, a strict separation of civil and religious matters. In *T.F. v Ireland* [1995] 1 I.R. 321 for instance, the High Court refused, in a case challenging the constitutionality of judicial separation laws, to hear testimony from a Catholic priest regarding matters of Roman Catholic canon law. Similarly, in *M.R. v T.R.* [2006] I.E.H.C. 359, McGovern J. noted that the concern of the courts is to enforce the law, and not morality, The courts moreover had no role in "weigh[ing] the views of one religion against another" or in resolving conflicts on points of morality (as opposed to law).

The ban on the endowment of religion

The Constitution generally precludes the State from funding or otherwise endorsing the propagation of religion or religious beliefs.

The "endowment" (the Irish text uses the term "maoiniú", which means the enhancement of wealth) of religion is prohibited by Art.44.2.2°. The State, or a local authority, could not, for instance, fund the erection of a religious statue or icon (such as a statue of Buddha, or a crucifix), or permit this to occur on public lands, as it would involve the endowment of religion.

That said, the decided cases on this issue tend to lean heavily in favour of allowing the State to support religious organisations in certain respects. For instance, in *Campaign to Separate Church and State v Minister for Education* [1998] 2 I.L.R.M. 181, the Supreme Court ruled as follows.

- It is permissible for the State to fund the provision of education in schools run by religious groups and orders. The Constitution appears implicitly to allow this when it states that the funding of schools shall not discriminate between schools run by different religious denominations (Art.44.2.4°). This suggests that the Constitution anticipated that the State would fund schools run by religious groups.
- It is possible for the State to pay for the provision of religion teachers in such schools. Because religious education is a fundamental part of the curriculum in religious run schools, and the State is entitled to fund education in such schools, the court concluded that the State was also allowed to fund religious instruction in denominational schools.
- It is permissible, moreover, for the State to pay the salaries of school chaplains, that is, ministers of religion charged with the religious formation and general moral welfare of students in a particular school.

Although this seems to run counter to Art.44.2.2°, the courts, in so ruling, appear to have endorsed a general legal trend in favour of supporting the practice of religion.

That said, where a school is being funded by the State, no child may be forced, against its parents wishes, to attend religious instruction in such a school (Art.44.2.4°). Similarly, a child cannot be excluded from a State-funded school on the grounds that such child will not be attending religious instruction.

The ban on religious discrimination

It is generally unconstitutional for the State, in its laws, to differentiate between people on the basis of their religious profession, status or belief.

Example: The State may not discriminate between persons on the grounds of their status within a particular religious grouping. In *Mulloy v Minister for Education* [1975] I.R. 88, a priest who had taught for some time in a school in Nigeria was, when he returned to Ireland, denied incremental salary credits (i.e. extra pay) in respect of this work. The sole reason for this denial was that the plaintiff was a priest. Had the plaintiff been a layperson teaching abroad, he would have been given incremental credit. This discriminatory treatment constituted a breach of Art.44.2.3°.

Example: The State cannot penalise a person for marrying outside his own religion. In *M. v An Bord Uchtála* [1975] I.R. 81, the High Court struck down a provision of the Adoption Act 1952 that prevented a couple of mixed faith from adopting a child.

Support for the practice of religion

The decided cases on freedom of religion seem generally to indicate a strong preference for the State support of religion, even where this may involve apparent infringements of the requirements of non-endowment and non-discrimination noted above.

Example: In *Quinn's Supermarket v Attorney General* [1972] I.R. 1, the Supreme Court declared unconstitutional a groceries order that exempted Jewish kosher shops from general restrictions on opening hours. (Kosher shops are facilities that prepare food in accordance with Jewish religious laws.) In doing so, however, the court concluded that had such an exemption been fully necessary to facilitate those of the Jewish faith in the free practice of their religion, the measure would have been constitutionally permissible. The court felt that the exemption went further than was necessary to protect the free practice of the Jewish faith (i.e. it was disproportionate). It did, however, agree that a less restrictive exemption, designed to ensure that Jewish people would not be forced to purchase their Sunday meat before sundown on a Saturday, the end of their Sabbath, would have been permissible. This was despite the fact that such a measure would technically have involved discrimination between different religions.

Example: In *McGrath v Maynooth College* [1979] I.L.R.M. 166, two lecturers were dismissed from their jobs at a State-funded Catholic third-level college because they had broken certain religious rules imposed by the Roman Catholic Church. The Supreme Court ruled that the dismissals were valid despite the fact that such a ruling involved an endorsement of the discriminatory rules of a particular religion. The court's reasoning in this regard again seemed to suggest that the State was entitled, even obliged, to support the free practice of religion, even where this involved turning a blind eye to the unfair practices of such religions. (See also *Flynn v Power* [1985] I.R. 648, where the High Court endorsed a decision of a religious order to dismiss a teacher who had become pregnant outside marriage.)

Example: In *Campaign to Separate Church and State v Minister for Education* [1998] 2 I.L.R.M. 181, the Supreme Court ruled that it was not unconstitutional to fund the salaries of religious chaplains working in State-run community schools. The reasoning of the court was that the State, in doing so, was merely supporting the free choice of parents regarding the religious formation of their children, as guaranteed by Art.42.4 of the Constitution.

Summary

Despite the specific provisions of Art.44 of the Constitution, the courts in Ireland have tended to rule in favour of measures that support and buttress the free practice of religion in Ireland. This seems to be the case even where such measures appear, on a literal interpretation, to infringe the ban on religious discrimination and the ban on the endowment of religion contained in Art.44.

Such reasoning is problematic. Mindful of the religious oppression and conflict that has blighted Ireland's history, Art.44.2 clearly and definitively bans both the endowment of religion and any form of discrimination between persons of different religious persuasion. It is at least arguable that such provisions require that the State be neutral in its attitude to religion and, in particular, to the propagation of religion in schools. It seems instead that the courts have taken a broad approach to the interpretation of the Constitution, preferring the overall religious sentiment of the constitutional document to the more specific provisions of Art.44.

23. AMENDING THE CONSTITUTION

Amending the Constitution

How is the Constitution amended?

Only the People of Ireland can amend the Constitution. They do so in referenda proposed by the Houses of the Oireachtas (see generally Arts 46 and 47). Such proposals are put to the People in the form of a "Bill" initiated in Dáil Éireann and passed (or deemed under Art.23 to have been passed) by both the Dáil and the Seanad. If the referendum proposal succeeds in attracting a majority of the votes cast in the referendum, the Amendment will be deemed to have passed. In such a case the President will sign and promulgate the Act as having amended the Constitution.

Between 1938 and 1941, it was possible for the Oireachtas on its own to amend the Constitution. It did so on two occasions, once in 1939 and again in 1941. The Constitution, however, expressly prevented the Oireachtas from using its power to change the Constitution to extend the period during which the Oireachtas enjoyed this power. Thus, this power to amend the Constitution is no longer available to the Oireachtas. Since 1941, only the People may make an amendment to the Constitution.

What kind of amendments can the People make?

The People may amend the Constitution in whatever way they see fit. There are no restrictions or limits on the type of amendments that can be effected (see the decision of the Supreme Court in *Re Article 26 and the Regulation of Information Bill 1995* [1995] 1 I.R. 1). The People could, for instance, pass an amendment that did little more than clarify the meaning of the Constitution. (See *Finn v Attorney General* [1983] I.R. 514).

The courts have consistently stressed that the manner in which the Constitution is amended is a matter for the People alone. The courts will not, moreover, entertain a request to clarify the meaning of a proposed amendment before it is passed by the People.

In particular, judges are extremely reluctant to prevent a referendum proposal passed by the Oireachtas from being put to the People. In a series of cases the courts have refused to stop a referendum proposed by the Oireachtas from being put to the People, the rationale being that the People are entitled to vote on any proposal that the Oireachtas puts to them (see, for instance, *Finn v Attorney General* [1983] I.R. 514, *Slattery v An Taoiseach* [1993] 1 I.R. 286 and *Riordan v An Taoiseach (No. 2)* [1999] 4 I.R. 343).

For instance, in *Morris and Ó Maoldhomhnaigh v Minister for the Environment* [2002] 1 I.R. 326, Kelly J. refused to prevent the Twenty-Fifth Amendment of the Constitution from being put to the People. The Amendment proposed to change the law on abortion, restricting abortions where the threat to the life of the mother was self-imposed, (thus preventing an abortion where the mother was suicidal as a result of her pregnancy). The Amendment stated further that the conditions under which a termination of pregnancy would be permitted would be contained in a proposed Bill, published alongside the Amendment, which the Oireachtas would pass if the Amendment itself passed. The plaintiffs complained that it was not permissible to change the Constitution by reference to a document outside the Constitution. The terms of the Bill, they argued, should have been incorporated into the Constitution itself. Rejecting this proposition, Kelly J. concluded that it was perfectly permissible for the People to give constitutional validity to a document by reference to it in the Constitution. In line with precedent, the judge noted that the People were entitled to change the Constitution in whatever way they saw fit.

The conduct of a referendum

While the courts generally will not interfere in relation to the substance of a proposal to amend the Constitution, they have, on several occasions, acted in relation to the manner in which a referendum is conducted. In particular, the courts have stressed the importance of equal treatment by the State of the campaigns for and against the amendment. It is illegal, according to the decision of the Supreme Court in *McKenna v An Taoiseach (No. 2)* [1995] 2 I.R. 10, for either the Government or the Oireachtas to spend public monies with a view to promoting the Government's official view on a referendum. In that case, the Supreme Court ruled that the allocation by the State of nearly €650,000 to promote a "Yes" vote in the divorce referendum of 1995 was unconstitutional, as it breached the guarantee of equality between citizens. Therefore:

- Where public funds are spent on a referendum campaign, both sides of the argument must be funded equally.
- In a similar vein, according to *Coughlan v RTÉ* [2000] 3 I.R. 1, the time allocated to a referendum debate by public sector broadcasters (such as RTÉ and TG4) cannot discriminate between the "yes" and "no" sides of the campaign.

The Amendments explained

To date, since 1937, there have been a total of 23 Amendments made to the Constitution, two by the legislature and the remainder by the People in referendum. Six referenda have proved unsuccessful, having been rejected by the People. The numbering of the Amendments may strike readers as odd. There is, for instance, no twelfth, twenty-fourth or twenty-fifth Amendments, the proposals for these changes having been turned down. A proposal for a twenty-second Amendment, regarding the removal and censure of judges, was proposed but withdrawn before referendum in 2001.

- *First Amendment, 1939:* Article 28.3 originally allowed for emergency legislation to be enacted (even if it infringed the terms of the Constitution) but only when the State was actually at war. The First Amendment, enacted on the outbreak of the Second World War, extended Art.28.3 to cover situations of conflict occurring outside the State in which the State itself is not a participant (see above at pp.23–25).
- *Second Amendment, 1941:* Introduced miscellaneous minor alterations, mainly to improve the Irish text of the Constitution.
- *Third Amendment, 1972:* Allowed Ireland to become part of the European Economic Community, the European Coal and Steel Community and the European Atomic Energy Community (Euratom) (see Ch.6 above).
- *Fourth Amendment, 1973:* Reduced the minimum voting age from 21 to 18 for Dáil and presidential elections.
- *Fifth Amendment, 1973:* When enacted, Art.44 contained a clause recognising "the special position of the Roman Catholic Church". In light of the divisive nature of this clause, the People voted to remove it in 1973.
- *Sixth Amendment, 1979:* Article 34 of the Constitution reserves to judges the task of administering justice. Amidst some legal concern that the decisions of the Adoption Board (an Bord

Uchtála) might be regarded as impinging upon this judicial function, the People provided that the Board's decisions could not be deemed invalid on the grounds that it was not a court.

- *Seventh Amendment, 1979:* Amends Art.18 of the Constitution. At the time, only graduates of the University of Dublin (Trinity College) and of the National University of Ireland could vote for the six university-elected Senators. The Seventh Amendment allows the State to redistribute the six seats amongst all third-level institutions as it sees fit. To date, however, the State has not used this provision.

- *Eighth Amendment, 1983:* Amidst concerns that the constitutional right to privacy might, as in the USA (see *Roe v Wade* 410 U.S. 113 (1973)), give rise to a right to an abortion, the People expressly confirmed the right to life of the unborn child, while also guaranteeing the equal right to life of its mother (see Ch.17 above).

- *Ninth Amendment, 1984:* In the Electoral Bill 1983 the Oireachtas sought to extend the right to vote in Dáil elections to British citizens resident in Ireland, on foot of reciprocal arrangements put in place in the UK for Irish citizens. In an Art.26 reference of the Bill (*In the Matter of the Electoral (Amendment) Bill* [1984] I.R. 268), this provision was found to be an infringement of Art.16.1, which reserved the right to vote to Irish citizens. The Ninth Amendment, however, altered Art.16 to allow for the extension of the vote to foreign nationals resident in Ireland, in appropriate circumstances.

- *Tenth Amendment, 1987:* Allowed Ireland to ratify the Single European Act, a measure designed to deepen the integration of the European Communities.

- *Eleventh Amendment, 1992:* Permitted Ireland to ratify the Treaty of Maastricht, establishing the European Union.

- *Thirteenth and Fourteenth Amendments, 1992:* These Amendments were put to the people as part of a package designed to deal with the fallout from *Attorney General v X.* [1992] 1 I.R. 1. The Thirteenth Amendment stipulates that the right to life of the unborn child cannot be invoked to prevent a woman from travelling to obtain an abortion lawfully available in a foreign country. The Fourteenth Amendment prohibits Art.40.3.3° (the Eighth Amendment) from being used to prevent information being distributed in this State concerning abortion lawfully available abroad, subject to certain conditions laid down in legislation (see the Regulation of Information Act 1995). (See Ch.17 above.)

• **Fifteenth Amendment, 1995:** Prior to 1995, Art.41.3.2° prevented Parliament from legislating for divorce. This effectively precluded already married parties from re-marrying on marital breakdown unless they could obtain a declaration to the effect that the marriage had never existed (i.e. a decree of nullity). By a slim majority, the People approved the introduction of limited divorce in 1995. An Irish court may now grant a divorce but only where the parties have been living apart for four of the previous five years. Additionally, the court must be satisfied that there is no prospect of reconciliation and that the parties have made proper provision for all family members (see above at pp.174–175).

• **Sixteenth Amendment, 1996:** Before this amendment, a person could be denied bail only where it was feared that he would either interfere with witnesses or seek to abscond from justice. The Sixteenth Amendment permitted the extension of the grounds for refusing bail to situations where it is feared that the accused will commit further crimes while on bail (see above at pp.109–111).

• **Seventeenth Amendment, 1997:** The principle of cabinet confidentiality, as set out in *Attorney General v Hamilton (No.1)* [1993] 2 I.R. 250, meant that the content of cabinet discussions could not be revealed, even in evidence given to a court of law or a tribunal. This amendment allowed the High Court to require the giving of evidence, where needed by a court of law or tribunal, notwithstanding the cabinet confidentiality rule (see above at pp.86–88).

• **Eighteenth Amendment, 1998:** Permitted Ireland to sign up to the Amsterdam Treaty (1997) amending the Treaties of the European Union and Communities.

• **Nineteenth Amendment, 1998:** Allowed the State to ratify the Good Friday Agreements (1998) securing a political settlement on the status and governance of Northern Ireland. This amendment, in particular, allowed Arts 2 and 3 of the Constitution to be changed, dropping the former legal claim over Northern Ireland, a broad aspiration to unity being inserted in its place. The State, moreover, acknowledged that the present status of Northern

Ireland (as part of the United Kingdom) would only change with the consent of a majority in both Ireland and Northern Ireland, and only by peaceful and democratic means (see Ch.4 above).

*   ***Twentieth Amendment, 1999:*** Provided the first constitutional recognition for the operation of local government, i.e. County and City Councils. It also required that local elections be held at least once every five years (see Art.28A).

*   ***Twenty-First Amendment, 2001:*** Comprehensively abolished for all purposes the State's right to order a sentence of death for a crime. Thus, "capital punishment" can no longer be exacted even under the authority of the emergency provisions of Art.28.3 (see Art.15.5.2).

*   ***Twenty-Third Amendment, 2001:*** Permitted the State to ratify an international treaty setting up the International Criminal Court of Justice.

*   ***Twenty-Sixth Amendment, 2002:*** Allowed the State to ratify the Nice Treaty, following an earlier rejection in a 2001 referendum. The Treaty made certain changes to the EU treaties with a view to permitting the expansion of the European Union.

*   ***Twenty-Seventh Amendment, 2004:*** Prior to this Amendment, any person born in the island of Ireland could claim citizenship. This Amendment allowed the Legislature to restrict citizenship to children at least one of whose parents is an Irish citizen. (See above at pp.17–39).

Can an amendment be made contingent on events occurring?

Yes. An amendment can contain a contingency or condition precedent to its activation. For instance, the Nineteenth Amendment (removing the legal claim over Northern Ireland) was stated to be conditional on an order of Government being made (in this case, following the establishment of the bodies agreed under the Good Friday agreement). Similarly, it appears that a constitutional amendment can refer to, and thus sanction a text that is external to the text of the Constitution (see *Morris*, discussed above).

The failed amendments

To date, six amendments have been unsuccessfully put before the People:

- Two amendments proposing the abolition of the system of proportional representation in Irish elections have both been rejected, one in 1959 and the other in 1968;
- A proposal to permit the introduction of divorce was defeated in 1986 (though a further proposal was subsequently successful in 1995);
- In 1992, the People rejected a proposal that would have prevented women from obtaining, on the grounds of a suicidal condition, an abortion in Ireland;
- In 2001, a proposal to ratify the Nice Treaty, which facilitated the expansion of the European Union, was defeated in a referendum; (If successful, this would have been termed the Twenty-Fourth Amendment)
- In March 2002, a referendum proposing to allow the Oireachtas to regulate the availability of abortion in Ireland by means of an Act of Parliament, the Protection of Human Life in Pregnancy Act 2002, was narrowly defeated in referendum. This legislation proposed to restrict the availability of abortion in cases where a mother of an unborn child threatened to take her own life unless she could obtain an abortion. (If successful, this would have been termed the Twenty-Fifth Amendment)

Can a referendum be put to the People more than once?

There is no restriction on a failed referendum being put to the People a second time. The ban on divorce and the Nice Treaty, for instance, have both been put to People twice, with the second referendum succeeding on each occasion. In the case of the Nice Treaty, the two referenda were held in consecutive years. While some might argue that this fails to respect the People's wishes, there is nothing in the Constitution to prevent a re-run of a failed referendum. Of course, the People are perfectly free to stand firm; indeed, the electorate has twice rejected similar attempts to restrict abortion and to remove the requirement of proportional representation in elections.

INDEX

1. F's Judgement sets out to have a commment to harmony, impartitiality, and interpretaion to make an appropriate constitutional decision.

2. F argues the 8th was anti abortion law. Meaning women can't have a dignity based rights to abortion

3. A womans con right to life includes a life without equality, privacy and diberty.

4. F attributes how particular circumstances eg. Rape pregnancy due to rape, have a larger burden on women

5. F beleves Given Circumstances X, more weight should be given to life of mother

6. Art 40.3.3 endorses a public duty to support reproductive life. Meaning the state cannot absolvate the whole burden to women. They must provide fair living conditions.